Agnes Strickland (1796–1874)
Lives of the Queens of England
(1840–1848)

Since 1969 Antonia Fraser has written many acclaimed, prizewinning historical works, which have also been international bestsellers. These include *Mary, Queen of Scots, Cromwell: Our Chief of Men, The Weaker Vessel: Women's Lot in Seventeenth-Century England,* and *Marie Antoinette: The Journey.* In 2010 she published a memoir of her life with Harold Pinter entitled *Must You Go?*

Antonia Fraser won a Wolfson History Prize in 1984, and was made CBE in 1999.

CONTINUUM HISTORIES

The greatest narrative history writing in English

This series is designed to attract a new
generation of readers to some of the greatest
narrative history ever written. Each volume includes a
dramatic episode from a major work of history, prefaced
with an introduction by a leading modern authority.

Continuum Histories demonstrate the
extraordinary tradition that exists of great history
writing in the English language – and that often
the best stories are true stories.

Series Editor: Mark Bostridge

Lives of
the Queens
of England

Also in Continuum Histories

William H. Prescott's *History of the Conquest of Mexico*.
Introduced and selected by J.H. Elliott

J.A. Froude's *The Reign of Mary Tudor*.
Introduced and selected by Eamon Duffy

Lord Macaulay's *History of England*.
Introduced and selected by John Burrow

Thomas Carlyle's *The French Revolution*.
Introduced and selected by Ruth Scurr

Edward Gibbon's *Decline and Fall of the Roman Empire*.
Introduced and selected by Tom Holland (forthcoming)

AGNES STRICKLAND'S

Lives of
the Queens
of England

Introduced and selected by
Antonia Fraser

continuum

Published by the Continuum International Publishing Group

The Tower Building   80 Maiden Lane
11 York Road   Suite 704
London   New York
SE1 7NX   NY 10038

www.continuumbooks.com

First published 2011

British Library Cataloguing-in-Publication Data
A catalogue record for this book is available from the British
Library.

ISBN 978-1441-10947-7

Designed and typeset by www.benstudios.co.uk
Printed and bound in India by Replika Press Pvt Ltd

CONTENTS

INTRODUCTION

Agnes Strickland achieved considerable fame in her lifetime for her multitudinous biographies, which tended to come in royal flushes like some elaborate game of cards. Besides the best-known *Lives of the Queens of England*, first published in twelve volumes between 1840 and 1848, she also embarked upon a number of other similar projects including *Lives of the Tudor Princesses*, *The Stuart Princesses*, and *Lives of the Queens of Scotland* (notable for its portrait of Mary Queen of Scots). There was even the *Lives of the Bachelor Kings of England*, a series which sounded more promising than it proved, for upon investigation there turned out to be a singular dearth of authentically unmarried sovereigns; and when Miss Strickland sent a copy of the work to the then bachelor Prince of Wales – the future Edward VII – he wrote back politely saying that he was sure she would not wish him to qualify for a future series of biographies of this title.

Yet this warm-hearted and romantic-minded spinster can fairly claim, as Dame Una Pope-Hennessy put it in her own biography of Agnes Strickland published in 1940, to have been as epoch-making in her way as Lytton Strachey was to be in his. She founded a whole new school of vivid utterly readable history, aimed to capture the general reader who felt himself inadequately served in the 1940s either by the pedantic scholar or the over-imaginative historical novelist. And, if the art of historical biography today is practised by the many – not the least of them women – it must be remembered that Agnes Strickland, a hundred and seventy years ago, was a pioneer. It was fitting that as an old lady when she went down to Oxford, Agnes Strickland should be acclaimed by the undergraduates with the merry cry: "The Queens! The Queens! Three cheers for the Queens!" For she was the first of what was to prove a long and flourishing line of lady biographers.

Agnes Strickland was born in 1796, one of six sisters out of a family of nine, brought up by her father mainly at home at Reydon Hall, near Southwold in Suffolk. As a country gentleman Thomas Strickland was hardly affluent, and his business connections brought him more trouble than money; but he did endow all his daughters with an excellent predominantly literary education, believing (unusually for the times) that the female mind should be strengthened if only to take part in rational conversation with men. The sisters thus nurtured in a Brontë-type nursery with home-made plays, stories and verses, remained devoted to each other throughout life: the especially close link of Agnes and her elder sister Elizabeth may be judged by the fact that *Lives of the Queens*, and indeed all the great historical series for which Agnes became famous, were in fact the composite work of the two sisters. As a method, each worked quite separately on their own subjects: thus out of the thirty-three English queens nineteen were the exclusive work of Elizabeth and fourteen that of Agnes – to Agnes falling the three Matildas, Eleanor of Provence, Isabella of France, Joanna of Navarre, Margaret of Anjou, Anne Boleyn, Anne of Cleves, Katherine Howard, Katharine Parr, Queen Elizabeth, Catharine of Braganza and Mary Beatrice of Modena.

The total concealment of Elizabeth's name from the title-page was the result of her own fervent wish for anonymity: and it was a happy arrangement since the gregarious and extrovert

Agnes much enjoyed the process of becoming a literary celebrity, leaving to her sister the more secret life of delving into archives. One can, I think, detect a certain difference in the styles of the two authoresses, seen most explicitly in their respective treatments of the consorts of Henry VIII, echoing the differences in their characters. Elizabeth had the drier, more hard-hitting style, while Agnes was the more colourful writer inclined to use sentiment as well as argument in appealing to her readers. Both sisters had published children's books separately before they collaborated on the mammoth *Lives*, the idea probably arising from some historical sketches of female sovereigns which Elizabeth had written for the *Court Magazine*. A commission was secured from a leading publisher, Henry Colburn, and permission secured to dedicate the *Lives* to the young female sovereign who had recently ascended the throne – Queen Victoria. Curiously enough, when the *Lives* first appeared, only Queen Victoria seems to have been acute enough to discern that they were in fact the work of two different pens.

The *Lives* themselves were an instantaneous success with the public, running through four editions by 1854, only six years after the series was completed; in 1864 11,000 copies of a new six-volume edition were sold, and sales continued steadily from then on. Unfortunately the Strickland sisters never seem to have made much money out of it themselves owing to an unsatisfactory deal with Colburn in the first place, and the muddled state of their finances may be judged by the fact that towards the end of her life Agnes was granted £100 a year out of the Civil List by Mr. Gladstone. But Agnes at least enjoyed to the full such social benefits as presentation in Queen Victoria's drawing-room, as well as a rich circle of friends who prized her "as a woman as well as an author" as another sister, Jane, proudly recalled. When an anonymous reviewer in *The Spectator* attacked Agnes spitefully for having turned to literature merely because her attempts to get married had proven fruitless, Agnes, said Jane, treated their comments with a lofty disdain (in which feminism and anti-feminism were however curiously mixed): "The infelicity of celebrated literary women in the married state forms a heavy list. That some exceptions may be found is certain; but, indeed, it cannot add to the comfort of a husband if his wife's time is so occupied. A female author is wiser to remain unmarried. . . ."

In what does the appeal of the *Lives* consist? For unlike some best-sellers of a bygone age, they remain in many ways as fresh and as entertaining as their first delighted readers must have found them. In the first place the *Lives* are definitely not founded on fantasy: the sisters did take enormous pains with their research and this at a time when the State Papers were not even calendared but lying about in unclassified bundles covered with the candle grease of former scholars; moreover when the State Paper Room was fully opened, women were barred and the Stricklands only effected entry against the declared wishes of Lord John Russell after a prolonged campaign of personal lobbying of other politicians. In France on the contrary they were much helped by the historian Guizot whom they had encountered as French Ambassador in London; certain lives in particular such as those of Catharine of Braganza and Mary of Modena, whose long and virtually unknown widowhoods were spent abroad, gained much value from this access to foreign archives. The Stricklands were also tireless in visiting the actual scenes of their heroines' lives, as a result of which much of the topographical detail is most successful, and many local traditions have been preserved.

Their friendship with the old English Catholic families just beginning to emerge from hibernation after Catholic Emancipation, to whom they were drawn by their family connections to the Queens they studied, enabled them to write of

Catholic sovereigns such as Henrietta Maria or Mary Tudor with an understanding rare in early Victorian England. Of course the Stricklands were not scholars as such, and Agnes in particular was sometimes lead by enthusiasm into sheer gullibility: of this blindness to the facts, her conviction that the signature of Queen Elizabeth to the death warrant of Mary Queen of Scots was actually forged is probably the most famous example. In reading these *Lives* one should therefore be wary of accepting any strikingly original historical judgement without reference to a more established authority.

The real strength of the Stricklands, which time has not diminished, lies in the wonderful sympathy which they were able to display for their heroines whatever their vicissitudes. To this was added much narrative skill, pointed up by their skilful use of anecdotes "forgotten or unknown" as the contemporary historical Lingard put it, commenting favourably on their works. Guizot himself paid them a Gallic compliment: "You have studied from the source and presented your facts singularly exempt from dryness." But above all it was this sympathy which gave and still gives them a wonderful universality. The sisters loved their work and they also loved their subjects. It was a powerful combination, and if not the only formula for successful biography, it is certainly one which remains likely to produce books highly pleasing to the reader, since under its spell each character springs to life once more; we suffer and rejoice again with ancient woes and ancient loves. When Agnes died in 1874, a year before the self-effacing Elizabeth, the inscription on her tombstone at Southwold read: "Historian of the Queens of England". It seems an appropriate epitaph for one who had dedicated herself to resurrecting from their own forgotten historical graves so many of their number. So long as the *Lives* are read, neither she nor they will be forgotten.

Antonia Fraser

SUGGESTIONS FOR FURTHER READING

M. Delorme, '"Facts not Opinions": Agnes Strickland', *History Today* (38), 1988.

A. Laurence, 'Women historians and documentary research: Lucy Aikin, Agnes Strickland, Mary Everett Green, and Lucy Toulmin Smith', *Women, scholarship and criticism*, ed. J. Bellamy, A. Laurence and G. Perry (Manchester University Press, 2000).

Rosemary Mitchell, *Picturing the Past, English history in text and image, 1830–1870*, (Oxford University Press, 2000).

Una Pope-Hennessy, *Agnes Strickland: Biographer of the Queens of England 1796–1874* (Chatto & Windus, 1940).

J. M. Strickland, *Life of Agnes Strickland* (W. Blackwood and sons, 1887).

LIVES OF
THE QUEENS
OF ENGLAND

THE FALL OF ANNE BOLEYN

Anne was now at the summit of human greatness. She had won the great political game for which she had, in the bitterness of disappointed love, vindictively entered the lists with the veteran statesman who had separated her from the man of her heart. She had had the vengeance she had vowed for the loss of Percy, and laid the pride and power of Wolsey in the dust. She had wrested the crown matrimonial from the brow of the royal Katharine. The laws of primogeniture had been reversed, that the succession to the throne might be vested in her issue, and the two men who were the most deservedly venerated by the king and the people of England, More and Fisher, had been sacrificed to her displeasure. But in all these triumphs there was little to satisfy the mind of a woman whose natural impulses were those of virtue, but who had violated the most sacred ties for the gratification of the evil passions of pride, vanity, and revenge. Anne Boleyn was a reader of the Scriptures, and must have felt the awful force of that text which says, "What shall it profit a man if he gain the whole world and lose his own soul?" Conscious of her own responsibility, and finding far more thorns than roses in the tangled weary labyrinth of greatness, Anne directed her thoughts to the only true source of happiness, religion, which had hitherto been practised by her rather as a matter of state policy than as the emanation from a vital principle in the soul. She became grave and composed in manner, and, ceasing to occupy herself in the gay pursuits of pleasure, or the boisterous excitement of the chase, spent her hours of domestic retirement with her ladies, as her royal mistress Katharine had formerly done before her, in needlework and discreet communication. Wyatt tells us, that the matchless tapestry at Hampton Court was for the most part wrought by the skilful hand of this queen and her ladies; "But far more precious," he says, "in the sight of God were those works which she caused her maidens and those about her daily to execute in shirts and other garments for the use of the poor; and not contented with that, her eye of charity, her hand of bounty passed through the whole land; each place felt that heavenly flame burning in her – all times will remember it."

The change that had taken place in the manners of Anne Boleyn and her court has been attributed to the influence of the celebrated reformer, Hugh Latimer. The queen had rescued this eloquent and zealous minister from the durance to which Stokesley, bishop of London, had committed him. But for the powerful protection of Anne, Latimer would, in all probability, have been called to testify the sincerity of his principles at the stake five-and-twenty years before he was clothed with the fiery robes of martyrdom. At her earnest solicitation the king interposed, and Latimer was restored to liberty. The queen next expressed a wish to see and hear the rescued preacher; and Latimer, instead of addressing his royal protectress in the language of servile adulation, reminded her of the vanity of earthly greatness and the delusions of human hopes and expectations. Anne listened with humility, and entreated him to point out whatever appeared amiss in her conduct and deportment. Latimer, in reply, seriously represented to her how much it behoved her, not only to impress the duties of morality and piety on her attendants, but to enforce her precepts by example. Anne, far from being offended at his sincerity, appointed him for one of her chaplains, and afterwards obtained his promotion to the see of Worcester. To her credit, it is also recorded, that she directed a certain sum, from her privy purse, to be distributed to every village in England for the relief of its distressed inhabitants. With greater wisdom she planned the institution of a variety of manufactures, with a view of giving more permanent assistance to those who were destitute of a livelihood, and without employment. For the last nine months of her life she distributed 14,000*l*. in alms; she also caused many promising youths to be educated, and sent to college, at her expense, with the intention of rendering their talents and learning serviceable in the church. In all these things Anne performed the duties of a good woman and an enlightened queen; and had she attained to her royal elevation in an honest and conscientious manner, in all probability the blessing of God would have been with her, and prospered her undertakings. But however powerful Anne's religious impressions might be, it is impossible that a real change of heart had taken place, while she continued to incite the king to harass and persecute his forsaken queen, Katharine, by depriving her of the solace of her daughter's company, and exacting from the disinherited princess submissions from which conscience and nature alike revolted. There were moments when Anne felt the insecurity of her position in a political point of view; and well must she have known how little reliance was to be placed on the stability of the regard of the man whose caprice had placed the queenly diadem on her brow. At the best, she was only the queen of a party, for the generous and independent portion of the nobles and people of England still regarded Katharine as the lawful possessor of the title and place which Henry had bestowed on her.

When the long-expected tidings of Katharine's death arrived, Anne, in the blindness of her exultation, exclaimed, "Now I am, indeed, a queen!"

It is said that she was washing her hands in a costly basin when sir Richard Southwell brought the intelligence to her, on which she instantly gave him both the basin and its rich cover as a reward for his tidings. The same evening she met her parents with a countenance full of pleasure, and bade them rejoice with her, for the crown was now firmly fixed on her head. On the day of her royal rival's funeral she not only disobeyed the king's order, which required black to be worn on that day, but violated good taste and good feeling alike by appearing in yellow, and making her ladies do the same. The change in Henry's feelings towards Anne may, in all probability, be attributed to the disgust caused by the indelicacy of her triumph. She had been ill and out of spirits previously to this event, which was attributed to the sufferings incidental to her condition, for she was again likely to become a mother; but after the death of queen Katharine she recovered her vivacity, and assumed so haughty a carriage that she offended every one.

The season was now at the hand when Anne was, in her turn, to experience some of the bitter pangs she had inflicted on her royal mistress. Her agonies were not the less poignant, because conscience must have told her that it was retributive justice which returned the poisoned chalice to her own lips, when she, in like manner, found herself rivalled and supplanted by one of her female attendants, the beautiful Jane Seymour. Jane must have been a person of consummate art; for she was on terms of great familiarity with the king before Anne entertained the slightest suspicion of their proceedings. Entering the room unexpectedly one day, the queen surprised Jane, seated on Henry's knee, receiving his caresses with every appearance of complacency. Struck, as with a mortal blow, at this sight, Anne gave way to a transport of mingled grief and indignation. Henry, dreading his consort's agitation might prove fatal to his hopes of an heir, endeavoured to sooth and reassure her, saying, "Be at peace, sweetheart, and all shall go well for thee." But the cruel shock Anne had sustained brought on the pangs of premature travail; and after some hours of protracted agony, during which her life was in imminent peril, she brought forth a dead son, January 29th.

When the king was informed of this misfortune, instead of expressing the slightest sympathy for the sufferings of his luckless consort, he burst into her apartment, and furiously upbraided her "with the loss of his boy."

Anne, with more spirit than prudence, passionately retorted, "that he had no one to blame but himself for this disappointment, which had been caused by her distress of mind about that wench, Jane Seymour."

Henry sullenly turned away, muttering, as he quitted her apartment, that "she should have no more boys by him."

These scenes, which occurred in January, 1536, may surely be regarded as the first act of the royal matrimonial tragedy, which four months later was consummated on Tower Hill.

Anne slowly regained her health, but not her spirits. She knew the king's temper too well not to be aware that her influence was at an end for ever, and that she must prepare to resign, not only her place in his affections, but also in his state, to the new star by whom she had been eclipsed. When she found that she had no power to obtain the dismissal of her rival from the royal household, she became very melancholy, and withdrew herself from all the gaieties of the court, passing all her time in the most secluded spots of Greenwich Park.

It is also related, that she would sit for hours in the quadrangle court of Greenwich Palace in silence and abstraction, or seeking a joyless pastime in playing with her little dogs, and setting them to fight with each other. The king had entirely withdrawn himself from her company ever since her rash retort to his unfeeling reproach, and now they never met in private. She had not the consolation of her infant daughter's innocent smiles and endearments to beguile her lonely sorrow, for the princess Elizabeth was nursed in a separate establishment, and the sweet tie of maternity had been sacrificed to the heartless parade of stately ceremonials. She had alienated the regard and acquired the enmity of her uncle Norfolk. Her royal sister-in-law and early patroness, Mary, queen of France, was no more, and Suffolk, Henry's principal favourite, was one of her greatest foes.

There is reason to believe that the queen had incurred the suspicion and displeasure of her royal husband early in the preceding year, by some mysterious intrigue with the cabinet of her old friend, Francis I., of which we find evidence in a curious despatch from Gontier, the French ambassador, dated February 5th, 1535, addressed to the admiral of France, with whom the queen was in correspondence. Gontier tells the admiral that he was introduced into queen Anne's apartment, where he found the king, and the lords and ladies of the court. She talked with him apart on the contents of the admiral's letter, with which she appeared greatly perplexed and dismayed. "She complained," said Gontier, "of my too long stay which had engendered in the king, her husband, many doubts and strange thoughts, for which, she said, there was a great need that you should devise some remedy on the part of the king, her brother [Frances I.], or that she was altogether lost and ruined; for she found she was herself in more trouble and annoy than she was before her nuptials; charging me, to pray and require (on her part) attention to her affair, of which she could not stay to speak to me so fully as she wished, for fear, both of the place where she then was and the eyes that were watching her countenance, not only of her said lord and husband, but of his nobles that were there." She told me "that she could neither write to me nor see me, nor could she stay with me longer. At which speech she left me to follow her lord, the king, into the next call, where the dances were forming without the said lady being there." Gontier adds, "My lord, this I cannot but know, that she is ill at ease, and I presume to say, on my poor judgement, that the doubts and suspicions of the king, which I mentioned before, have caused her this trouble."

A strange scene is here unveiled in Anne Boleyn's queenly life, in which we see her acting her part in terror and perplexity, and confiding to the plenipotentiary of a foreign sovereign her apprehensions lest her royal husband should detect her double dealings. Yet this aside was ventured in the presence of Henry, and before the very courtiers whose observing eyes she dreaded. Such situations are sometimes represented on the stage indeed, but even there appear too highly touched with romance.

The inconsistency of Anne Boleyn's manners was, doubtless, the principle cause of her calamities. The lively, coquettish maid of honour could not forget her old habits, after her elevation to a throne; and the familiarity of her deportment to those with whom she had formerly been on terms of equality in the court of queen Katharine encouraged her officers of state to address her with undue freedom. Such was her unbound thirst for admiration, that even the low-born musician Mark Smeaton dared to insinuate his passion to her. These things were, of course, reported to her disadvantage by the household foes by whom she was surrounded. The king's impatience to rid himself of the matrimonial fetters which precluded him from sharing his throne with the object of his new passion would not brook delays, and, in the absence of any proof of the queen's disloyalty to himself, he resolved to proceed against her on the evidence of the invidious gossips' tales, that had been whispered to him by persons who knew that he was seeking an occasion to destroy her. Three gentlemen of the royal household, Brereton, Weston, and Norris, with Mark Smeaton, the musician, were pointed out as her paramours; and as if this had not been enough, the natural and innocent affection that subsisted between Anne and her only brother George, viscount Rochford, was construed into a presumption of a crime of the most revolting nature. This dreadful accusation proceeded from the hatred and jealousy of Lady Rochford, who, being in all probability an ill-assorted companion for her accomplished husband, regarded his friendship and confidential intercourse with the queen, his sister, with those malignant feelings of displeasure which prompted her murderous denunciation of them both.

The secret plot against the queen must have been organised by the first week in April, 1536; for on the 4th of that month the parliament was dissolved, as if for the purpose of depriving her of any chance of interference from that body in her behalf. The writs for the new parliament, which was to assemble on the 8th of June, after her death, were issued even before she was arrested, April 27th. Three days before that date, a secret committee was appointed of the privy council to inquire into the charges against her. Among the commissioners were her uncle, the duke of Norfolk, the duke of Suffolk, the lord chancellor, her father, several earls, and some of the judges. It has been supposed that her father did not attend. William Brereton was summoned before this committee on Thursday, the 28th, and, after his examination, was committed to the Tower.

Two days afterwards, the queen (who was totally unconscious of this portentous circumstance) found Mark Smeaton, the musician, standing in the round window of her presence-chamber in a melancholy attitude. She asked him, "why he was so sad?" "It is no matter," he replied.

Then the queen had the folly to say, "You may not look to have me speak to you as if you were a nobleman, because you be an inferior person." "No, no, madam," he replied, "a look sufficeth me."

There can be little doubt that Mark's sadness was caused by the fearful rumours that must have reached him of the arrest of Brereton, the proceedings of the queen's enemies in council, and the general aspect of affairs at court; and that he was loitering in the window for the purpose of giving his royal mistress a hint of the peril that threatened her. The absurd vanity, which led her to attribute his troubled looks to a hopeless passion for herself, gave, perhaps, a different turn to the conversation, and diverted him from his purpose.

The next day the wretched man was arrested, sent to the Tower, and loaded with irons.

If the queen remained in ignorance of what was going on in the palace, as most authors affirm, her powers of observation must have been very limited, and she could have had no faithful friend or counsellor immediately about her.

The only reason we have to surmise that Anne was aware of the gathering storm is, that a few days before her arrest she held a long private conference with her chaplain, Matthew Parker, and gave him a solemn charge concerning the infant princess Elizabeth, it may be supposed regarding her religious education. This fact is authenticated in a letter from Parker to one of Elizabeth's councillors, declining the archbishopric of Canterbury, in which he says, "Yet he would fain serve his sovereign lady in more respects than his allegiance, since he cannot forget what words her grace's mother said to him not six days before her apprehension."

On Monday, May 1st, an evil May-day for her, Anne Boleyn appeared for the last time in the pride and pomp of royalty, with her treacherous consort, at the jousts at Greenwich. Her brother, viscount Rochford, was the principal challenger, and Henry Norris was one of the defenders. In the midst of the pageant, which was unusually splendid, the king rose up abruptly and quitted the royal balcony, with a wrathful countenance, attended by six of his confidential followers. Every one was amazed, but the queen appeared especially dismayed, and presently retired.

The sports broke up, and lord Rochford and Henry Norris were arrested at the barrier on the charge of high treason; sir Francis Weston was taken into custody at the same time. The popular version of the cause of this public outbreak of Henry's displeasure is, that the queen, either by accident or design, dropped her handkerchief from the balcony at the feet of Norris, who, being heated with the course, took it up, and presumptuously wiped his face with it; he then handed it to the queen on the point of his lance; at which Henry changed colour, started from his seat, and retired in a transport of jealous fury, and gave the orders for the arrest of the queen and all the parties who had fallen under suspicion of sharing her favours.

It is very possible that the circumstances actually occurred as related above, and that Henry, who was anxiously awaiting an opportunity for putting his long-meditated project against the queen into execution, eagerly availed himself of the first pretext with which her imprudent disregard of the restraints of royal etiquette furnished him, to strike the blow. Without speaking to the queen, the king rode back to Whitehall, attended by only six persons, among whom was his devoted prisoner Norris, who had hitherto stood so high in his favour, that he was the only person whom he ever permitted to follow him into his bedchamber; Norris had been, as we have mentioned, one of the three witnesses of Henry's secret marriage with Anne. On the way, Henry rode with Norris apart, and earnestly solicited him to obtain mercy by acknowledging his guilt; Norris stoutly maintained his innocence, and that of the queen, nor would he consent to be rendered an instrument in her ruin. When they reached Westminster he was despatched to the Tower.

The public arrest of her brother and his luckless friends struck a chill to the heart of the queen, but of the nature of their offence, and that she was herself to be involved in the horrible charges against them, she remained in perfect unconsciousness till the following day. She sat down to dinner at the usual hour, but the meal passed over with uneasiness, for she took the alarm when she found that the king's waiter came out not with his majesty's wonted compliment of "much good may it do you." Instead of this greeting, she observed a portentous silence among her ladies, and that her servants stood about, with their eyes glazed with tears and downcast looks, which inspired her with dismay and strange apprehensions. Scarcely was the *surnap* removed, when the duke of Norfolk, with Audley, Cromwell, and others of the lords of the council, entered. At first, Anne thought they came from the king to comfort her for her brother's arrest, but when she noticed the austerity of their countenances, and the ominous presence of sir William Kingston, the lieutenant of the Tower, behind them, she started up in terror, and demanded "why they came." They

28

replied, with stern brevity, "that they came by the king's command to conduct her to the Tower, there to abide during his highness's pleasure."

"If it be his majesty's pleasure," replied the queen, regaining her firmness, "I am ready to obey;" and so pursues our authority, "Without change of habit, or any thing necessary for her removal, she committed herself to them, and was by them conducted to her barge." It is, however, certain, from the evidence of Kingston's letters, that she underwent a harsh examination before the council at Greenwich before her embarkation, unless the cruel treatment, which she complained of receiving from her uncle Norfolk on that occasion, took place in the barge, where, it is said, she was scarcely seated, ere he entered into the subject of her arrest, by telling her "that her paramours had confessed their guilt." She protested her innocence vehemently, and passionately implored to be permitted to see the king that she might plead her own cause to him. To all her asseverations of innocence the duke of Norfolk replied with contemptuous ejaculations.

It was on the 2nd of May that Anne was brought as a woeful prisoner to her former royal residence – the Tower. Before she passed beneath its fatal arch she sunk upon her knees, as she had previously done in the barge, and exclaimed, "Oh Lord, help

me, as I am guiltless of that whereof I am accused!"
Then perceiving the lieutenant of the Tower, she
said, "Mr. Kingston, do I go into a dungeon?" "No,
madam," said he, "to your own lodging, where you
lay at your coronation."

The recollections associated with that event
overpowered her, and, bursting into a passion of
tears, she exclaimed, "It is too good for me. Jesus,
have mercy on me!" She knelt again, weeping
apace, "and, in the same sorrow, fell into a great
laughter," – laughter more sad than tears. After the
hysterical paroxysm had had its way, she looked
wildly about her, and cried, "Wherefore am I here,
Mr. Kingston?"

The clock was just on the stroke of five when
Anne entered the Tower. The lords, with the
lieutenant, brought her to her chamber, where
she again protested her innocence: then, turning
to the lords, she said, "I entreat you to beseech
the king in my behalf, that he will be good lord
unto me;" as soon as she had uttered these words
they departed. "She desired me," says Kingston, "to
move the king's highness, that she might have the
sacrament in her closet, that she might pray for mercy,"
asseverating, at the same time, in the strongest
terms, her innocence of having wronged the king.
"I am the king's true wedded wife," she added, and

then said, "Mr. Kingston, do you know wherefore I am here?" "Nay," replied he; then she asked, "When saw you the king?" "I saw him not since I saw him in the tilt-yard," said he. "Then, Mr. Kingston, I pray you to tell me where my lord Rochford is?" Kingston answered, "I saw him before dinner in the court." "Oh! where is my sweet brother?" she exclaimed. The lieutenant evasively replied, "That he saw him last at York Place" (Whitehall Palace), which it seems was the case. "I hear say," continued she, "that I shall be accused with three men, and I can say no more than – nay. Oh, Norris, hast thou accused me? Thou art in the Tower, and thou and I shall die together; and Mark, thou art here too! Oh, my mother, thou wilt die for sorrow!" Then, breaking off from that subject, she began to lament the dangerous state into which lady Worcester had been thrown by the shock of hearing of her arrest. Interrupting herself again, she exclaimed, "Mr. Kingston, shall I die without justice?" "The poorest subject the king hath has that," replied the cautious official. A laugh of bitter incredulity was her only comment.

The unfortunate queen was subjected to the insulting presence and cruel espionage of her greatest enemy, lady Boleyn, and Mrs. Cosyns, one of her ladies, who was equally disagreeable

to her. These two never left her either by day or
night, for they slept on the pallet at the foot of
her bed, and reported even the delirious ravings
of her hysterical paroxysms to those by whom
her fate was to be decided. They perpetually
tormented her with insolent observations, and
annoyed her with questions, artfully devised,
for the purpose of entangling her in her talk,
or drawing from her own lips admissions that
might be turned into murderous evidence of her
guilt. She complained "that they would tell her
nothing of my lord, her father," for whose fate
she was evidently apprehensive. She expressed
a wish to be served in her prison by the ladies
of her privy chamber whom she favoured most,
and concluded by defying her aunt. Lady Boleyn
retorted in these words, "The desire and partiality
you have had for such tale-bearers has brought
you to this."

Mrs. Cosyns impertinently asked the queen,
"Why Norris had told her almoner on the preceding
Saturday, that he could swear the queen was a good
woman?" "Marry," replied Anne, "I bade him do so,
for I asked him, 'Why he did not go on with his
marriage?' and he made answer 'that he would
tarry awhile.' 'Then,' said I, 'you look for dead men's
shoes; if aught but good should come to the king

(who was then afflicted with a dangerous ulcer), you would look to have me;' he denied it, and I told him, 'I could undo him if I would,' and thereupon we fell out." This conversation (if it be really true, that Anne had the folly to repeat it to persons of whose deadly hatred she was so fully aware, and whom she knew were placed about her as spies) will impress every one with the idea, that she must have been on very perilous terms with Norris, if she allowed him to hold such colloquies with her. No one, however, seems to have considered the possibility of the whole of this deposition being a false statement on the part of the spies who were employed to criminate her. It seems scarcely credible that a woman of Anne Boleyn's age and long experience in public life would thus commit herself by unnecessary avowals, tending to furnish evidence against herself, of having imagined the death of the king, her husband.

Anne betrayed a humane, but certainly imprudent care for the comforts of the unhappy gentlemen who were in durance for her sake, by inquiring of lady Kingston, "Whether any body made their beds?" "No, I warrant you," was lady Kingston's familiar reply. The queen said, "that ballads would be made about her:" and as far as may be judged from the defaced passages in the MS., added, "that none could do that better than Wyatt." "Yes," said lady Kingston, "master Wyatt, – you have said true."

The next day, Kingston reported the queen's earnest desire to have the eucharist in her closet, and also to see her almoner. Devett is the name of him whom she desired, but Cranmer was appointed by Henry. Her mind was variously passioned that day. "One hour," says her gaoler, "she is determined to die, and the next hour much contrary to that." "Yesterday," continues he, "I sent for my wife, and also for mistress Cosyns, to know how she had done that day, and they said she had been very merry, and made a great dinner, and yet soon after called for her supper, having marvel 'where I was all day.' At my coming she said, 'Where have you been all day?' I made answer, and said, 'I had been with the prisoners.' 'So,' said she, 'I thought I heard Mr. Treasurer.' I assured her he was not here. Then she began to talk, and said, 'I was cruelly handled at Greenwich with the king's council, with my lord of Norfolk; who said, 'Tut, tut, tut,' shaking his head three or four times. 'As for my lord treasurer,' she said, 'he was in Windsor Forest all the time.'" This was her father.

Thus in Kingston's letters to Cromwell, her minutest sayings are detailed; but it is to be observed, that he often speaks from the reports of her pitiless female tormentors. He states, "That the queen expressed some apprehension of what Weston might say in his examination, for that he had told her on Whit-monday last, 'that Norris came more into her chamber for her sake than for Madge,' one of her maids of honour." By way of postscript, Kingston adds, "Since the making of this letter, the queen spake of Weston, that she had told him he did love her kinswoman, Mrs. Skelton, and that he loved not his wife; and he answered again, 'That he loved one in her house better than them both.' She asked him, 'Who?' to which he replied, 'Yourself,' on which she defied him."

When they told her Smeaton had been laid in irons, she said, "that was because he was a person of mean birth, and the others were all gentlemen." She assured Kingston, "That Smeaton had never been but once in her chamber, and that was when the king was at Winchester, and she sent for him to play on the virginals; for there," said she, "my lodging was above the king's." She related, also, what had passed between her and Smeaton on the Saturday before his arrest. Her passionate love for music, in which she herself greatly excelled, had undoubtedly led her to treat this person with a greater degree familiarity than was becoming in a queen.

There were times when Anne would not believe that Henry intended to harm her, and, after complaining that she was cruelly handled, she added, "But I think the king does it to prove me;" and then she laughed, and affected to be very merry. Merriment more sad than tears, reminding us of

"Moody madness, laughing wild
Amidst severest woe."

Reason must indeed have tottered when she predicted that there would be no rain in England till she was released from her unmerited thraldom. To this wild speech Kingston familiarly rejoined, "I pray then it be shortly, because of the dry weather, you know what I mean." "If she had her bishops, they would plead for her," she said.

Cranmer, from whom she probably expected most, wrote in the following guarded strain to Henry on the subject:

"If it be true what is openly reported of the queen's grace, if men had a right estimation of things, they should not esteem any part of your grace's honour to be touched thereby, but her honour only to be clearly disparaged.

And I am in such a perplexity, that my mind is clean amazed, for I never had a better opinion in woman than I had had of her, which maketh me think that she should not be culpable. Now I think that your grace best knoweth, that next unto your grace I was most bound unto her of all creatures living. Wherefore I must humbly beseech your grace to suffer me in that which both God's law, nature, and her kindness, bindeth me, unto that I may (with your grace's favour) wish and pray for her. And from that condition your grace, of your only mere goodness, took her, and set the crown upon her head, I repute him not your grace's faithful servant and subject, nor true to the realm, that would not desire the offence to be without mercy punished, to the example of all others. And as I loved her not a little, for the love I judged her to bear towards God and his holy Gospel, so, if she be proved culpable, there is not one that loveth God and his Gospel that will ever favour her, but must hate her above all other, and the more they love the Gospel, the more they will hate her, for then there never was creature in our time that so much slandered the Gospel. And God hath sent her this punishment, for that she feignedly hath professed the Gospel in her mouth, and not in her heart and deed, and though she hath offended, so that she hath deserved never to be reconciled to your grace's favour, yet God Almighty hath manifoldly declared his goodness towards your grace, and never offended you."

The letter concludes with an exhortation to the king not to think less of the Gospel on this account. The letter is dated from Lambeth, May 3rd. Cranmer adds a postscript, stating, "That the lord-chancellor and others of his majesty's house had sent for him to the Star-Chamber, and there declared such things as the king wished him to be shewn, which had made him lament that such faults could be proved on the queen as he had heard from their relation."

Anne entreated Kingston to convey a letter from her to Cromwell, but he declined so perilous a service. She was at times like a newly caged eagle in her impatience and despair. "The king wist what he did," she said bitterly, "when he put such women as my lady Boleyn and Mrs. Cosyns about her." She had two other ladies in attendance on her in her doleful prison-house, of more compassionate dispositions we may presume, for they were not allowed to have any communication with her, except in the presence of Kingston and his wife, who slept at her chamber door. Her other ladies slept in an apartment further off. One of these, we think, must have been Mary, the sister of her early and devoted friend, sir Thomas Wyatt. Among the few faithful hearts whose attachment to Anne Boleyn survived the awful changes in her fortunes, were those of Wyatt and his sister.

Wyatt is supposed to have had a narrow escape from sharing the fate of the queen, her brother, and their fellow-victims. It is certain that he was at this period under a cloud; and in one of his sonnets, he significantly alludes "to the danger which *once* threatened him in the month of May," – the month which proved so fatal to queen Anne. Very powerful was the sympathy between them; for, even when a guarded captive in the Tower, Anne spake with admiration of Wyatt's poetical talents. It was probably by the aid of his sister that Anne, on the fourth day of her imprisonment, found means to forward the following letter, through Cromwell's agency, to the king:

"Your grace's displeasure and my imprisonment are things so strange unto me, that what to write, or what to excuse, I am altogether ignorant. Whereas you sent to me (willing me to confess a truth and so obtain your favour), by such a one, whom you know to be mine ancient professed enemy; I no sooner received this message by *him*, than I rightly conceived your meaning; and if, as you say, confessing a truth indeed may procure my safety, I shall, with all willingness and duty, perform your command. But let not your grace ever imagine that your poor wife will ever be brought to acknowledge a fault, where not so much as thought ever proceeded. And to speak a truth, never a prince had wife more loyal in all duty, and in all true affection, than you have ever found in Anne Bolen, – with which name and place I could willingly have contented myself in God and your grace's pleasure had so been pleased. Neither did I at any time so far forget myself in my exaltation, or received queenship, but that I always looked for such alteration as I now find; for the ground of my preferment being on no surer foundation than your grace's fancy, the least alteration was fit and sufficient (I knew) to draw that fancy to some other subject.

"You have chosen me from a low estate to be your queen and companion, far beyond my desert or desire; if then you found me worthy of such honour, good your grace, let not any light fancy or bad counsel of my enemies withdraw your princely favour from me, neither let that stain – that unworthy stain – of a disloyal heart towards your good grace, ever cast so foul a blot on me and on the infant princess your daughter [Elizabeth].

"Try me, good king, but let me have a lawful trial, and let not my sworn enemies sit as my accusers and as my judges; yea, let me receive an open trial, for my truth shall fear no open shames; then shall you see either mine innocency cleared, your suspicions and conscience satisfied, the ignominy and slander of the world stopped, or my guilt openly declared. So that whatever God and you may determine of, your grace may be freed from an open censure, and mine offence being so lawfully proved, your grace may be at liberty, both before God and man, not only to execute worthy punishment on me, as an unfaithful wife, but to follow your affection already settled on that party, for whose sake I am now as I am; whose name I could some good while since, have pointed unto; – your grace being not ignorant of my suspicion therein.

"But if you have already determined of me, and that not only my death, but an infamous slander, must bring you the joying of your desired happiness, then I desire of God that he will pardon your great sin herein, and, likewise, my enemies, the instruments thereof, and that he will not call you to a strait account for your unprincely and cruel usage of me at his general judgement-seat, where both you and myself must shortly appear; and in whose just judgement, I doubt not (whatsoever the world may think of me) mine innocency shall be openly known and sufficiently cleared.

"My last and only request shall be, that myself may only bear the burden of your grace's displeasure, and that it may not touch the innocent souls of those poor gentlemen, whom, as I understand, are likewise in strait imprisonment for my sake.

"If ever I have found favour in your sight – if ever the name of Anne Bulen have been pleasing in your ears – then let me obtain this request; and so I will leave to trouble your grace any further: with mine earnest prayer to the Trinity to have your grace in his good keeping, and to direct you in all your actions.

"From my doleful prison in the Tower, the 6th of May.

"ANN BULEN."

The authenticity of this beautiful letter has been impugned for various reasons, but chiefly because the handwriting differs from the well-known autographs of Anne Boleyn. But the fact that it was found among Cromwell's papers four years after her death proves it to be a contemporary document.

The cautious but pathetic indorsement, "To the King, from the ladye in the Tower," identifies it, no less than the peculiar nature of the contents, as the composition of the captive queen. The original, we may reasonably suppose, had been forwarded to the king by Mr. Secretary Cromwell. The only real objection which occurs to us is, that the letter is signed "Ann Bulen" instead of *"Anna the quene."*

It is, however, possible, in the excited state of feeling under which this passionate appeal to the fickle tyrant was written, that his unfortunate consort fondly thought, by using that once beloved signature, to touch a tender chord in his heart. But the time of sentiment, if it ever existed with Henry, was long gone by; and such a letter from a wife whom he had never respected, and had now ceased to love, was more calculated to awaken wrath than to revive affection. Every word is a sting envenomed by the sense of intolerable wrong. It is written in the tone of a woman who has been falsely accused; and imagining herself strong in the consciousness of her integrity, unveils the guilty motives of her accuser, with a reckless disregard to consequences, perfectly consistent with the character of Anne Boleyn.

Her appeal in behalf of the unfortunate gentlemen who were involved in her calamity is generous, and looks like the courage of innocence. A guilty woman would scarcely have dared to allude to the suspected partners of her crime. It is strange that the allusion to the infant Elizabeth in this letter is made without any expression of maternal tenderness.

On the 10th of May, an indictment for high treason was found, by the grand jury of Westminster, "against the lady Anne, queen of England; George Boleyn, viscount of Rochford; Henry Norris, groom of the stole; sir Francis Weston and William Brereton, gentlemen of the privy chamber; and Mark Smeaton, a performer on musical instruments, a person specified as of low degree, promoted for his skill to be a groom of the chambers." The four commoners were tried, in Westminster Hall, May 10, by a commission of oyer and terminer, for the alleged offences against the honour and the life of their sovereign. A true bill had been found against them by the grand juries of two counties, Kent as well as Middlesex, because some of the offences specified in the indictment were said to have taken place at Greenwich, others at Hampton Court, and elsewhere.

Smeaton endeavoured to save his life by pleading guilty to the indictment. He had previously confessed, before the council, the crime with which he and the queen were charged. The three gentlemen, Norris, Weston, and Brereton, resolutely maintained their innocence, and that of their royal mistress, though urged by every persuasive, even the promise of mercy, if they would confess. They persisted in their plea, and were all condemned to death. On what evidence they were found guilty no one can now say, for the records of the trial are not in existence; but in that reign of terror English liberty and English law were empty words. Almost every person whom Henry VIII. brought to trial for high treason was condemned, as a matter of course; and at last he omitted the ceremony of trials at all, and slew his noble and royal victims by acts of attainder *ad libitum*.

Every effort was used to obtain evidence against Anne from the condemned prisoners, but in vain.

"No one," says sir Edward Baynton, in his letters to the treasurer, "will accuse her, but *alonely* Mark, of any actual thing." How Mark's confession was obtained becomes an important question as to the guilt or innocence of the queen. Constantine, whose testimony is any thing but favourable to Anne Boleyn, says, "that Mark confessed, but it was reported that he had been grievously racked first." According to Grafton, he was beguiled into signing the deposition which criminated himself, the queen, and others, by the subtlety of the admiral, Sir William Fitzwilliam, who, perceiving his hesitation and terror, said, "Subscribe, Mark, and you will see what will come of it." The implied hope of preserving a dishonoured existence prevailed. The wretched creature signed the fatal paper, which proved the death-doom of himself as well as his royal mistress. He was hanged that he might tell no tales. Norris was offered his life if he would confess, but declared "that he would rather die a thousand deaths than accuse the queen of that of which he believed her, in his conscience, innocent." When this noble reply was reported to the king, he cried out, "Hang him up then, hang him up!"

On the 16th of May, queen Anne and her brother, lord Rochford, were brought to trial in a temporary building which had been hastily erected for that purpose within the great hall in the Tower. There were then fifty-three peers of England, but from this body a selected moiety of twenty-six were named by the king as "lords triers," under the direction of the duke of Norfolk, who was created lord high steward for the occasion, and sat under the cloth of state. His son, the earl of Surrey, sat under him as deputy earl marshal. The duke's hostility to his unfortunate niece had already betrayed him into the cruelty of brow-beating and insulting her in her examination before the council at Greenwich. It has been erroneously stated by several writers that Anne's father, the earl of Wiltshire, was one of the "lord triers," but this was not the case. The duke of Suffolk, one of her determined enemies, was one of her judges, so also was Henry's natural son, the duke of Richmond, who had married her beautiful cousin the lady Mary Howard, the daughter of the duke of Norfolk. This youth as well as Suffolk, as a matter of course, voted according to the king's pleasure. The earl of Northumberland, Anne's first lower, was named on the commission for her trial. He appeared in his place, but was taken suddenly ill, the effect, no doubt, of violent agitation, and quitted the court before the arraignment of the lord Rochford, which preceded that of the queen. He died a few months afterwards.

Lady Rochford outraged all decency, by appearing as a witness against her husband. The only evidence adduced in proof of the crime with which he was charged, was, that one day, when making some request to his sister, the queen, he leaned over her bed, and was said by the by-standers to have kissed her.

He defended himself with great spirit and eloquence, so that his judges were at first divided, and had the whole body of the peers been present, he might have had a chance of acquittal; but as we have shewn, the lords triers were a number selected by the crown for this service. The trial was conducted within strong walls, the jurors were picked men, and by their verdict the noble prisoner was found guilty. After he was removed, Anne queen of England was called into court by a gentleman usher.

She appeared immediately in answer to the summons, attended by her ladies and lady Kingston, and was led to the bar by the lieutenant and the constable of the Tower. The royal prisoner had neither counsel nor adviser of any kind, but she had rallied all the energies of her mind to meet the awful crisis; neither female terror nor hysterical agitation were perceptible in that hour. The lord of Milherve tells us, "that she presented herself at the bar, with the true dignity of a queen, and curtsied to her judges, looking round upon them all without any sign of fear." Neither does it appear that there was any thing like parade or attempt at theatrical effect in her manner, for her deportment was modest and cheerful. When the indictment was read, which charged her with such offences as never Christian queen had been arraigned for before, she held up her hand courageously, and pleaded "not guilty." She then seated herself in the chair which had been provided for her use while the evidence against her was stated.

Of what nature the evidence was, no one can now form an opinion, for the records of the trial have been carefully destroyed. Burnet affirms that he took great pains in searching for documents calculated to throw some light on the proceedings, and the chief result of his labours was an entry made by sir John Spelman, in his private note-book, supposed to have been written on the bench, when he sat as one of the judges before whom Norris, Weston, Brereton, and Smeaton, were tried for the alleged offences in which they had been, as it was said, participators with the queen. These are the words quoted by Burnet: "As for the evidence of the matter it was discovered by the lady Wingfield, who had been a servant to the queen, and, becoming suddenly infirm before her death, did swear this matter to one of her" . . . . Here the page containing the important fact communicated by the dying lady is torn off, and with it all the other notes the learned judge had made on these mysterious trials were destroyed; so that, and Burnet has observed, the main evidence brought against the queen and her supposed paramours was the oath of a dead woman, and that, we may add, on hearsay evidence. Crispin's account of the origin of the charge is, "That a gentleman reproving his sister for the freedom of her behaviour, she excused herself by alleging the example of the queen, who was accustomed," she said, "to admit sir Henry Norris, sir Francis Weston, master Brereton, Mark Smeaton the musician, and her brother lord Rochford, into her chamber, at improper hours," adding "that Smeaton could tell a great deal more."

The crimes of which the queen was arraigned were, that she had wronged the king her husband, at various times, with the four persons above named, and also with her brother lord Rochford. That she had said to each and every one of those persons that the king never had her heart. That she privately told each, separately, "that she loved him better than any person in the world," which things tended to the slander of her issue by the king. To this was added "a charge of conspiring against the king's life." In an abstract from the indictment printed in the notes of Sharon Turner's Henry VIII., the days on which the alleged offences were committed are specified. The first is with Norris, and is dated October 6th, 1533, within a month after the birth of the princess Elizabeth, which statement brings its own refutation, for the queen had not then quitted her lying-in chamber.

"For the evidence," says Wyatt, "as I never could hear of any, small I believe it was. The accusers must have doubted whether their *proofs* would not prove their *reproofs*, when they durst not bring them to the light in an open place." Every right-thinking man must indeed doubt the truth of accusations, which cannot be substantiated according to the usual forms of justice. The queen defended her own cause with ready wit and great eloquence. Wyatt says, "It was reported without the doors, that she had cleared herself in a most wise and noble speech." Another of the floating rumours that were in circulation among the people, before the event of her trial was publicly known, was, that having a quick wit and being a ready speaker, the queen did so answer all objections, that her acquittal was expected; "And," says bishop Godwin, "had the peers given their verdict according to the expectation of the assembly, she had been acquitted, but through the duke of Suffolk, one wholly given to the king's humour, they did pronounce her guilty." The decision of the peers is not required, like the verdict of a jury, to be unanimous, but is carried by a majority. If all had voted, no doubt she would have been saved. After the verdict was declared, the queen was required to lay aside her crown and other insignia of royalty, which she did without offering an objection, save that she protested her innocence of having offended against the king.

This ceremony was preparatory to her sentence, which was pronounced by her uncle, the duke of Norfolk, as lord high steward of England and president of the court commissioned for her trial. She was condemned to be burnt or beheaded at the king's pleasure. Anne Boleyn heard this dreadful doom without changing colour or betraying the slightest symptom of terror, but when her stern kinsman and judge had ended, she clasped her hands, and, raising her eyes to heaven, made her appeal to a higher tribunal, in these words: "Oh Father! Oh Creator! Thou who art the way, the life, and the truth, knowest whether I have deserved this death." Then, turning to her earthly judges, she said, "My lords, I will not say your sentence is unjust, nor presume that my reasons can prevail against your convictions. I am willing to believe that you have sufficient reasons for what you have done, but then they must be other than those which have been produced in court, for I am clear of all the offences which you then laid to my charge. I have ever been a faithful wife to the king, though I do not say I have always shewn him that humility which his goodness to me and the honour to which he raised me merited. I confess I have had jealous fancies and suspicions of him which I had not discretion and wisdom enough to conceal at all times. But God knows, and is my witness, that I never sinned against him in any other way. Think not I say this in the hope to prolong my life. God hath taught me how to die, and he will strengthen my faith. Think not that I am so bewildered in my mind as not to lay the honour of my chastity to heart now in mine extremity, when I have maintained it all my life long, as much as ever queen did. I know these my last words will avail me nothing, but for the justification of my chastity and honour. As for my brother and those others who are unjustly condemned, I would willingly suffer many deaths to deliver them; but, since I see it so pleases the king, I shall willingly accompany them in death, with this assurance, that I shall lead an endless life with them in peace." Then, with a composed air, she rose up, made a parting salutation to her judges, and left the court as she had entered it. Such is the graphic account that has been preserved of Anne Boleyn's looks, words, and demeanour, on this trying occasion, by a foreign contemporary, who was one of the few spectators who were permitted to witness it.

The lord mayor, who was present at the arraignment of Anne Boleyn, said afterwards, that "*he* could not observe any thing in the proceedings against her, but that they were resolved to make an occasion to get rid of her." As the chief judge in the civic court of judicature, and previously as an alderman of the city of London, this magistrate had been accustomed to weigh evidences and pronounce judgements on criminal causes, therefore his opinion is of importance in this case.

Camden tells us that the spectators deemed Anne innocent, and merely circumvented. This accords with the lord mayor's opinion. Smeaton was not confronted with her, and, as far as can be gathered of the grounds of her condemnation, it must have been on his confession only. It is said she objected "that one witness was not enough to convict a person of high treason," but was told "that in *her* case it *was* sufficient."

In these days the queen would have had the liberty of cross-questioning the witness against her, either personally or by fearless and skilful advocates. Moreover, it would have been in her power to have summoned even her late attendant, mistress Jane Seymour, as one of her witnesses. The result of that lady's examination might have elicited some curious facts. After her trial, Anne was conveyed back to her chamber, the lady Boleyn, her aunt, and lady Kingston, only attending her.

On the 16th of May, Kingston wrote in the following methodical style to Cromwell, on the subject of the dreadful preparations for the execution of the death-doomed queen and her brother:

"Sir

"This day I was with the king's grace, and declared the petitions of my lord of Rochford, wherein I was answered. Sir, the said lord much desireth to speak with you, which toucheth his conscience much, *as he saith*, wherein I pray you that I may know your pleasure, for because of my promise made unto my said lord to do the same; and also I shall desire you further to know the king's pleasure touching the queen, as well for her comfort, as for the preparations of scaffolds and other necessaries concerning. The king's grace shewed me that my lord of

Canterbury should be her confessor, and he
was here this day with the queen. And note
that in that matter, sir, the time is short, for
the king supposeth the gentlemen to die to-
morrow, and my lord Rochford, with the rest
of the gentlemen, are yet without confession,
which I look for, but I have told my lord
Rochford, that he be in a readiness to-morrow
to suffer execution, and so he accepts it very
well, and will do his best to be ready."

The same day on which this letter was written
the king signed the death-warrant of his once
passionately loved consort, and sent Cranmer
to receive her last confession. Anne appeared to
derive comfort and hope from the primate's visit
– hope, even of life; for she told those about her,
"that she understood she was to be banished, and
she supposed she should be sent to Antwerp."

Cranmer was aware of Henry's wish of dissolving
the marriage with Anne Boleyn, in order to
dispossess the little princess Elizabeth of the place
she had been given in the succession, and he had
probably persuaded the unfortunate queen not
to oppose his majesty's pleasure in that matter.
The flattering idea of a reprieve from death must
have been suggested to Anne, in order to induce

her compliance with a measure so repugnant to her natural disposition and her present frame of mind. When she was brought as a guarded prisoner from Greenwich to the Tower, she had told the unfriendly spectators of her disgrace, "that they would not prevent her from dying their queen," accompanying these proud words with a haughty gesticulation of her neck. Yet we find her, only the day after her conference with the archbishop, submitting to resign this dearly prized and fatally purchased dignity without a struggle.

She received, May 17th, a summons to appear, "on the salvation of her soul, in the archbishop's court at Lambeth, to answer certain questions as to the validity of her marriage with the king." Henry received a copy of the same summons; but as he had no intention of being confronted with his unhappy consort, he appeared by his old proctor in divorce affairs, Dr. Sampson. The queen, having no choice in the matter, was compelled to attend in person, though a prisoner under sentence of death. She was conveyed privately from the Tower to Lambeth.

The place where this strange scene, in the closing act of Anne Boleyn's tragedy, was performed, was, we are told, a certain low chapel or crypt in Cranmer's house at Lambeth, where, as primate of England, he sat in judgement on the validity of her marriage with the king. The unfortunate queen went through the forms of appointing doctors Wotton and Barbour as her proctors, who, in her name, admitted the pre-contract with Percy, and every other objection that was urged by the king against the legality of the marriage. Wilkin and some others have supposed that Anne submitted to this degradation as the only means of avoiding the terrible sentence of burning.

Cranmer pronounced "that the marriage between Henry and Anne was null and void, and always has been so." Cromwell was present in his capacity of vicar-general, and Heylin says, the sentence was pronounced by him.

Thus did Henry take advantage of his former jealous tyranny in preventing the fulfilment of Percy's engagement with Anne, by using it as a pretext against the validity of her marriage with himself, and this, too, for the sake of illegitimating his own child. With equal injustice and cruelty, he denied his conjugal victim the miserable benefit, which her degradation from the name of his wife and the rank of his queen appeared to offer her, namely, an escape from the sentence which had been passed upon her for the alleged crime of adultery; to which, if she were not legally his wife, she could not in law be liable. But Henry's vindictive purpose against her was evident from the beginning, and nothing would satisfy him but her blood. If he had insisted on the invalidity of their union as early as May 13th, when Percy was required to answer, whether a contract of marriage did not exist between him and the queen? Anne could not have been proceeded against on the charges in her indictment, and the lives of the five unfortunate men, who were previously arraigned and sentenced on the same grounds, would have been preserved as well as her own. In that case, she could only have been proceeded against as marchioness of Pembroke, and on a charge of conspiring against the life of the king; but as it does not appear that the slightest evidence, tending to establish that very improbable crime, was set forth, the blood of six victims would have been spared, if the sentence on the marriage had passed only three days before it did. Percy, however, denied on oath to the duke of Norfolk, the lord chancellor and others, that any contact was between him and the queen, though he had verbally confessed to cardinal Wolsey, "that he was so bound in honour to Anne Boleyn, that he could not in conscience marry another woman." It is probable that Anne's haughty spirit, as well as her maternal feelings, had also prompted her to repel the idea of a divorce with scorn till the axe was suspended over her. Perhaps she now submitted, in

59

the fond hope of preserving not only her own life, but that of her beloved brother, and the three gallant and unfortunate gentlemen who had so courageously maintained her innocence through all the terrors and temptations with which they had been beset.

If so, how bitter must have been the anguish which rent her heart, when the knell of these devoted victims, swelling gloomily along the banks of the Thames, reached her ears as she returned to her prison, after the unavailing sacrifice of her own and her daughter's rights had been accomplished at Lambeth! That very morning her brother and the other gentlemen were led to execution, a scaffold having been erected for that purpose on Tower Hill. Rochford exhorted his companions "to die courageously," and entreated those who came to see him suffer, "to live according to the gospel, not in preaching, but in practice," saying, "he would rather have one good liver, according to the gospel, than ten babblers." He warned his old companions of the vanity of relying on court favour and the smiles of fortune, which had rendered him forgetful of better things. As a sinner, he bewailed his unworthiness, and acknowledged the justice of his punishment in the sight of God, but the king "he said he had never offended, yet he prayed for him that he might have a long and happy life." He forgave all his enemies, and prayed "that he also might be forgiven by all whom he had injured." Then kneeling down, he calmly submitted his neck to the axe. By some writers it has been regarded as a proof of the queen's guilt, that her brother neither attempted to exonerate himself or her from the horrible offence with which they had been branded. But an innocent man might, with equal delicacy and dignity, have been silent on such a subject before such an audience. The accusation, if false, was properly treated with the contempt its grossness merited.

There is, however, a reason for lord Rochford's silence which has never been adduced by historians. He had made most earnest supplication for his life, and even condescended to entreat the intercession of his unworthy wife with the king to prolong his existence; and as Henry was no less deceitful than cruel, it is possible that he might have tempted Rochford with false hopes to admit the justice of his sentence. General professions of unworthiness and lamentations for sin on the scaffold were customary with persons about to suffer the sentence of the law; even the spotless and saint-like lady Jane Grey expressed herself in a similar strain. Therefore, as sir Henry Ellis observes, "no conclusions, as to the guilt of the parties accused, can reasonably be drawn from such acknowledgments."

Norris, Weston, and Brereton, taking their cue from Rochford's form of confession, made general acknowledgments of sinfulness, and requested the bystanders to judge the best of them.

Sir Francis Weston was a very beautiful young man, and so wealthy that his wife and mother offered to purchase his life of the king at the ransom of 100,000 crowns. Henry rejected both the piteous supplication and the bribe.

Mark Smeaton, being of ignoble birth, was hanged. He said, "Masters, I pray you all to pray for me, for I have deserved the death." This expression is considered ambiguous, for either he meant that he had committed the crime for which he was to die or that he merited his punishment for having borne false witness against his royal mistress. It was however reported, even at the time, that Mark Smeaton's confession was extorted by the rack, and that he was not confronted with the queen, lest he should retract it. Anne evidently expected that he would make the *amende* on the scaffold; for when she was informed of the particulars of the execution and his last words, she indignantly exclaimed, "Has he not then cleared me from the public shame he hath done me? Alas! I fear his soul will suffer from the false witness he hath borne. My brother and the rest are now, I doubt not, before the face of the greater King, and I shall follow to-morrow."

The renewed agony of hope, which had been cruelly and vainly excited in the bosom of the queen by the mockery of declaring that her marriage with the sovereign was null and void, appears soon to have passed away. She had drunk of the last drop of bitterness that mingled malice and injustice could infuse into her cup of misery; and when she received the awful intimation, that she must prepare herself for death, she met the fiat like one who was weary of a troublesome pilgrimage, and anxious to be released from its sufferings. Such are the sentiments pathetically expressed in the following stanzas, which she is said to have composed after her condemnation, when her poetical talents were employed in singing her own dirge.

"Oh, death, rock me asleep,
    Bring on my quiet rest,
Let pass my very guiltless ghost
    Out of my careful breast.
Ring out the doleful knell,
Let its sound my death tell;
        For I must die,
        There is no remedy,
        For now I die!

"My pains who can express,
 Alas! they are so strong!
My dolour will not suffer strength
 My life for to prolong
Alone in prison strange!
  I wail my destiny;
  Woe worth this cruel hap, that I
  Should taste this misery.

"Farewell my pleasures past,
 Welcome my present pain,
I feel my torments so increase
 That life cannot remain.
Sound now the passing bell,
Rung is my doleful knell,
For its sound my death doth tell.
  Death doth draw nigh,
  Sound the knell dolefully
  For now I die!"

There is an utter abandonment to grief and desolation in these lines which, in their rhythm and cadence, shew musical cultivation in the composer. Of a more prosaic nature, yet containing literal truths, as to the events to which they allude, are the verses she wrote after her return from her trial.

"Defiled is my name, full sore
  Through cruel spite and false report,
That I may say for evermore,
  Farewell to joy, adieu comfort.

"For wrongfully he judge of me;
  Unto my name a mortal wound,
Say what ye list, it may not be,
  Ye seek for that shall not be found."

Anne was earnest in preparing herself for death, with many and fervent devotional exercises; and whatever may have been said in disparagement by catholic historians, it is certain that she did not die a protestant. She passed many hours in private conference with her confessor, and received the sacraments according to the doctrine of transubstantiation. The penance she imposed upon herself for her injurious treatment of her royal step-daughter, the rememberance of which lay heavily upon her mind, when standing upon the awful verge of eternity, is most interestingly recorded by Speed, who quotes it from the relation of a nobleman:

"The day before she suffered death, being attended by six ladies in the Tower, she took the lady Kingston into her presence chamber, and there, locking the door upon them, willed her to sit down in the chair of state. Lady Kingston answered, 'that it was her duty to stand and not sit at all in her presence, much less upon the seat of state of her the queen.' 'Ah! madam,' replied Anne, 'that title is gone; I am a condemned person, and by law have no estate left me in this life, but for clearing my conscience; I pray you sit down.' 'Well,' said lady Kingston, 'I have often played the fool in my youth, and, to fulfil your command, I will do it once more in mine age;' and thereupon sat down under the cloth of estate on the throne. Then the queen most humbly fell on her knees before her, and, holding up her hands with tearful eyes, charged her, as in the presence of God and his angels, and as she would answer to her before them when all should appear to judgment, that she would want so fall down before the lady Mary's grace, her daughter-in-law, and, in like manner, ask her forgiveness for the wrongs she had done her; for, till that was accomplished,' she said, 'her conscience could not be quiet.'"

This fact is also recorded in Kingston's letters to Cromwell, but not so circumstantially as in the account quoted by Speed, from which we learn that Anne Boleyn continued to occupy her royal apartments in the Tower, (with the presence chamber and canopied chair of state), commonly called the queen's lodgings, and that she had the free range of them, even after the warrant for her execution was signed, although tradition points out more than one dismal tower of the royal fortress as the place of her imprisonment.

The queen was ordered for execution on the 19th of May; and it was decreed by Henry that she should be beheaded on the green within the Tower. It was a case without precedent in the annals of England; for never before had female blood been shed on the scaffold; even in the Norman reigns of terror, woman's life had been held sacred, and the most merciless of the Plantagenet sovereigns had been too manly, under any provocation or pretence, to butcher ladies. But the age of chivalry was over, and not one spark of its ennobling spirit lingered in the breast of the sensual tyrant who gave the first example of sending queens and princesses to the block, like sheep to the shambles. Perhaps there were moments when the lovely and once passionately beloved Anne Boleyn doubted the possibility of his consigning her to the sword of the executioner; that Henry was aware that his doing so would be an outrage on public decency is certain by his ordering all strangers to be expelled from the Tower. There is an expression in Kingston's letter with implies that a rescue was apprehended;

at any rate, the experiment was yet to be tried, how Englishmen would brook the spectacle of seeing their beautiful queen mangled by a foreign headsman, that the sovereign might be at liberty to bestow her place on her handmaid. As it was the king's pleasure that his conjugal victim should be decollated with a sword, after the French manner of execution, the headsman of Calais was brought over to England for the purpose, a man who was considered remarkably expert at his horrible calling. The unfortunate queen was duly apprised of this circumstance, with the other preparations for the last act of the tragedy that was to terminate her brilliant but fatal career. She had had mournful experience of the vanity and vexation of all the distinctions that had flattered her; beauty, wealth, genius, pleasure, power, royalty, had all been hers, and whither had they led her?

On Friday, the 19th of May, the last sad morning of her life, Anne rose two hours after midnight, and resumed her devotions with her almoner. Her previous desire of having the consecrated elements remain *in her closet*, (which in such a case is always for the purposes of adoration), and the fact that she termed the sacrament "the good Lord," proves plainly that she did not die a protestant. When she was about to receive the sacrament, she sent for sir William Kingston, that he might be a witness of her last solemn protestation of her innocence of the crimes for which she was sentenced to die, before she became partaker of the holy rite. It is difficult to imagine any person wantonly provoking the wrath of God by incurring the crime of perjury at such a moment. She had evidently no hope of prolonging her life, and appeared not only resigned to die, but impatient of the unexpected delay of an hour or two before the closing scene was to take place. This delay was caused by the misgivings of Henry, for Kingston had advised Cromwell not to fix the hour for the execution, so that it could be exactly known when it was to take place, lest it should draw an influx of spectators from the city.

It does not appear that Anne condescended to implore the mercy of the king. In her letter on the 6th of May, she had appealed to his justice, and reminded him that "he must hereafter expect to be called to a strict account for his treatment of her, if he took away her life on false and slanderous pretences;" but there is no record that she caused a single supplication to be addressed to him in her behalf. She knew his pitiless nature too well even to make the attempt to touch his feelings after the horrible imputations with which he had branded her, and this lofty spirit looks like the pride of innocence, and the bitterness of a deeply wounded mind.

While Kingston was writing his last report to Cromwell of her preparations for the awful change that awaited her, she sent for him, and said, "Mr. Kingston, I hear I shall not die afore noon, and I am very sorry therefore, for I thought to be dead by this time, and past my pain." "I told her," says Kingston, "that the pain should be little, it was so subtle;" and then she said, "I have heard say the executioner is very good, and I have a little neck," and put her hands about it, laughing heartily. "I have seen men and also women executed, and they have been in great sorrow," continues the lieutenant of the Tower, "but to my knowledge, this lady hath much joy and pleasure in death. Sir, her almoner is continually with her, and hath been since two o'clock after midnight." There must have been one powerful tie to bind the hapless queen to a world from which she appeared eager to be released. She was a mother, and was leaving her infant daughter to the domination of the treacherous beauty who was to take her place in Henry's state, as she had already done in his fickle fancy; and Anne Boleyn had no reason to expect that Jane Seymour would prove a kinder step-dame to Elizabeth than she had done to the princess Mary: an agonising thought in the hour of death. It is not known whether Anne requested to see her little one, who was quite old enough to know her and to return her caresses; for Elizabeth was at the attractive age of two years and eight months; but if the unfortunate queen preferred such a petition, it was fruitless, and she was led to the scaffold without being permitted to bestow a parting embrace on her child. Perhaps, she felt that such an interview would unfit her for acting her part in the last trying scene that awaited her with the lofty composure which its publicity required.

That great historian, lord Bacon, assures us that queen Anne protested her innocence with undaunted greatness of mind at the time of her death. He tells us, "that by a messenger, faithful and generous as she supposed, who was one of the king's privy chamber, she, just before she went to execution, sent this message to the king: 'Commend me to his majesty, and tell him he hath been ever constant in his career of advancing me; from a private gentlewoman he made me a marchioness, from a marchioness a queen, and now he hath left no higher degree of honour, he gives my innocency the crown of martyrdom.' But the messenger durst not carry this to the king, then absorbed in a new passion, yet tradition has truly transmitted it to posterity."

This sarcastic message is noted as a memorandum on the letter which Anne wrote to Henry from the Tower, probably by Cromwell or his secretary, and it has frequently been quoted by historians; but lord Bacon is the only person who places it in its apparently true chronology, the day of her death, when hope was gone, and the overcharged heart of the victim dared to give vent to its last bitterness in those memorable words.

The time appointed by Henry for the execution of his unhappy consort was twelve o'clock at noon. This was kept a profound mystery from the people till the time was at hand. A few minutes before that hour, the fatal portals through which the royal victim was to pass for the last time were thrown open, and she appeared dressed in a robe of black damask, with a deep white cape falling over it on her neck. She wore the pointed black velvet hood, which is familiar to us in her portraits; or, as some have said, a small hat with ornamented coifs under it; perhaps the picturesque bangled hat which forms part of the costume of her statue at Blickling Hall. The feverish state of excited feeling in which she had passed the morning vigil, had probably recalled the brightness to her eyes, and a flush to her cheek, which supplied the loss of her faded bloom; for she is said to have come forth in fearful beauty: indeed, one writer says, "Never had the queen looked so beautiful before." She was led by the lieutenant of the Tower, and attended by the four maids of honour who had waited upon her in prison. She was conducted by sir William Kingston to the scaffold, which was erected on the green before the church of St. Peter ad Vincula. Having been assisted by sir William to ascend the steps of the platform, she there saw assembled the lord mayor, and some of the civic dignitaries, and her great enemy the duke of Suffolk, with Henry's natural son, the duke of Richmond, who had, in defiance of all decency and humanity, come thither to disturb her last moments with their unfriendly espionage, and to feast their eyes upon her blood.

There also was the ungrateful blacksmith-secretary of state, Cromwell: who, though he had been chiefly indebted to her patronage for his present greatness, had shewn no disposition to succour her in her adversity. The fact was, his son and heir was married to the sister of Jane Seymour, Henry's bride-elect, and the climbing *parvenu* was one of the parties most interested in the fall of queen Anne, and affixing the stigma of illegitimacy on her daughter, for the advancement of his family connexion to the throne. Anne must have been perfectly aware of his motives, but she accorded him and the other reptilia of the privy council the mercy of her silence when she met them on the scaffold. She came there, as she with true dignity observed, "to die, and not to accuse her enemies." When she had looked round her, she turned to Kingston, and entreated him "not to hasten the signal for her death till she had spoken that which was on her mind to say;" to which he consented, and she then spoke: "Good Christian people, I am come hither to die, according to law, for by the law I am judged to die, and therefore I will speak nothing against it. I am come hither to accuse no man, nor to speak any thing of that whereof I am accused, as I know full well that aught that I could say in my defence doth not appertain unto you, and that I could draw no hope of life from the same. But I come here only to die, and thus to yield myself humbly unto the will of my lord the king. I pray God to save the king, and send him long to reign over you, for a gentler or more merciful prince was there never. To me he was ever a good and gentle sovereign lord. If any person will meddle with my cause, I require them to judge the best. Thus I take my leave of the world and of you, and I heartily desire you all to pray for me."

She then with her own hands removed the hat and collar, which might impede the action of the sword, and taking the coifs from her head delivered them to one of her ladies. Then covering her hair with a little linen cap (for it seems as if her ladies were too much overpowered with grief and terror to assist her, and that she was the only person who retained her composure), she said, "Alas! poor head, in a very brief space thou wilt roll in the dust on the scaffold; and as in life thou didst not merit to wear the crown of a queen, so in death thou deservest not better doom than this."

All present were then in tears, save the base court of sycophants, who came to flatter the evil passions of the sovereign. Anne took leave of her weeping ladies in these pathetic words:

"And ye, my damsels, who, whilst I lived, ever shewed yourselves so diligent in my service, and who are now to be present at my last hour and mortal agony, as in good fortune ye were faithful to me, so even at this my miserable death ye do not forsake me. And as I cannot reward you for your true service to me, I pray you take comfort for my loss; howbeit, forget me not, and be always faithful to the king's grace, and to her whom, with happier fortune, ye may have as your queen and mistress. And esteem your honour far beyond your life; and, in your prayers to the Lord Jesu, forget not to pray for my soul."

Among these last true followers of the unfortunate queen, was the companion of her childhood, Mrs. Mary Wyatt, sir Thomas Wyatt's sister, who, faithful through every reverse, attended her on the scaffold. To this tried friend Anne Boleyn gave, as a parting gift, her last possession, a little book of devotions, bound in gold, and enamelled black, which she had held in her hand from the time she left her apartment in the Tower till she commenced her preparations for the block. Mary always wore this precious relic in her bosom. Some mysterious last words, supposed to be a message to sir Thomas Wyatt, the queen was observed to whisper very earnestly to Mrs. Mary Wyatt, before she knelt down.

It was said that Anne refused to allow her eyes to be covered, and that, whenever the executioner approached her, his purpose was disarmed by his encountering their brilliant glances, till, taking off his shoes, he beckoned to one of the assistants to advance on one side as he softly approached on the other, and when the queen, deceived by this subterfuge, turned her eyes in the direction whence she heard the steps, he struck her head off with one blow of the Calais sword. The account given by the

Portuguese spectator of this mournful scene is as follows:

"And being minded to say no more, she knelt down upon both knees, and one of her ladies covered her eyes with a bandage, and then they withdrew themselves some little space, and knelt down over against the scaffold, bewailing bitterly and shedding many tears. And thus, and without more to say or do, was her head struck off; she making no confession of her fault, but saying, 'O Lord God, have pity on my soul.'"

This being the record of an eye-witness we think it is deserving of credit, and it agrees with the dignified composure of Anne's behaviour on the scaffold. Gratian says she died with great resolution, and so sedately as to cover her feet with her garments, in like manner as the Roman poet records of the royal Polyxena, when about to be sacrificed at the tomb of Achilles. According to another authority, her last words were, "*In manus tuas*." "The bloody blow came down from his trembling hand who gave it," says Wyatt, "when those about her could not but seem to themselves to have received it upon their own necks, she not so much as shrinking at it."

Spelman has noted that Anne Boleyn's eyes and lips were observed to move when her head was held up by the executioner. It is also said, that before those beautiful eyes sunk in the dimness of death, they seemed for an instant mournfully to regard her bleeding body as it fell on the scaffold.

It does not appear that the last moments of Anne were disturbed by the presence of lady Boleyn and Mrs. Cosyns. The gentler females, who, like ministering angels, had followed their royal mistress to her doleful prison and dishonouring scaffold, half-fainting and drowned in tears as they were, surrounded her mangled remains, now a spectacle appalling to woman's eyes; yet they would not abandon them to the ruffian hands of the executioner and his assistants, but, with unavailing tenderness, washed away the blood from the lovely face and glossy hair, that scarcely three years before had been proudly decorated with the crown of St. Edward, and now, but for these unbought offices of faithful love, would have been lying neglected in the dust. Our Portuguese authority informs us, "that one weeping lady took the severed head, the others, the bleeding body of the unfortunate queen and, having reverentially covered them with a sheet, placed them in a chest which there stood ready, and carried them to the church, which is within the Tower, where," continues he, "they say she lieth buried with the others," meaning, by her fellow-victims, who had two days before preceded her to the scaffold. There is, however, some reason to doubt whether the mangled remains of this hapless queen repose in the place generally pointed out in St. Peter's church, of the Tower, as the spot where she was interred. It is true, that her warm and almost palpitating form was there conveyed in no better coffin than an old elm-chest that had been used for keeping arrows, and there, in less than half-an-hour after the executioner had performed his part, thrust into a grave that had been prepared for her by the side of her murdered brother. And there she was interred, without other obsequies than the whispered prayers and choking sobs of those true-hearted ladies who had attended her on the scaffold, and were the sole mourners who followed her to the grave. It is to be lamented that history has only preserved one name out of this gentle sisterhood, that of Mary Wyatt, and all were worthy to have been inscribed in golden characters in every page sacred to female tenderness and charity. In Anne Boleyn's native county, Norfolk, a curious tradition has been handed down from father to son, for upwards of three centuries, which affirms that her remains were secretly removed from the Tower church under cover of darkness, and privately conveyed to Salle church, the ancient burial-place of the Boleyns, and there interred at midnight, with the holy rites that were denied to her by her royal husband at her first unhallowed funeral. A plain black marble slab, without any inscription, is still shewn in Salle church as a monumental memorial of this queen, and is generally supposed, by all classes of persons in that neighbourhood, to cover her remains.

The mysterious sentence with which Wyatt closes his eloquent memorial of the death of this unfortunate queen, affords a singular confirmation of the local tradition of her removal and re-interment: "God," says he, "provided for her corpse *sacred burial*, even in a place as it were consecrate to innocence."

This expression would lead us to infer, that Wyatt was in the secret, if not one of the parties who assisted in the exhumation of Anne Boleyn's remains, if the romantic tradition we have repeated be, indeed, based on facts. After all there is nothing to violate the probability in the tale, romantic though it be. King Henry, on the day of his queen's execution, tarried no longer in the vicinity of his metropolis than till the report of the signal gun, booming faintly through the forest glade, reached his ear, and announced the joyful tidings that he had been made a widower. He then rode off at fiery speed to his bridal orgies at Wolf Hall. With him went the confidential myrmidons of his council, caring little, in their haste to offer their homage to the queen of the morrow, whether the mangled remains of the queen of yesterday were securely guarded in the dishonoured grave into which they had been thrust, with indecent haste, that noon.

There was neither singing nor saying for her, no chapel *ardente* nor midnight requiem, as for other queens; and, in the absence of these solemnities, it was easy for her father, for Wyatt, or even for his sister, to bribe the porter and sextons to the church, to connive at the removal of the royal victim. That old elm-chest would excite no suspicion, when carried through the dark narrow streets and the Aldgate portal of the city, to the eastern road. It probably passed as a coffer of stores for the country, no one imagining that such a receptacle inclosed the earthly relics of their crowned and anointed queen.

It is remarkable, that in the ancient church of Horndon-on-the-hill, in Essex, a nameless black marble monument is also pointed out by village antiquaries as the veritable monument of this queen. The existence of a similar tradition of the kind in two different countries, but in both instances in the neighbourhood of sir Thomas Boleyn's estates, can only be accounted for on the supposition, that rumours of the murdered queen's removal from the Tower chapel were at one time in circulation among the tenants and dependents of her paternal house, and were them orally transmitted to their descendants as a matter of fact.

The execution of the viscount Rochford rendered his two sisters the coheiresses of their father, the earl of Wiltshire. The attainder of Anne Boleyn, together with Cranmer's sentence on the nullity of her marriage with the king, had, by the law of the land, deprived her and her issue of any claim on the inheritance of her father. Yet, on the death of the earl of Wiltshire, king Henry, in defiance of his own acts, did, with equal rapacity and injustice, seize Hever Castle and other portions of the Boleyn patrimony, in right of his divorced and murdered wife Anne, the elder daughter, reserving for her daughter Elizabeth all that Mary Boleyn and her heirs could otherwise have claimed.

Greenwich Palace was Anne Boleyn's favourite abode of all the royal residences. The park is planted and laid out in the same style as her native Blickling, and with the same kind of trees. It s natural to suppose that the noble intersected arcades of chestnuts, which form the principal charm of the royal park, were planted under the direction of this queen, in memory of those richer and luxuriant groves beneath whose blossomed branches she sported in careless childhood with her sister Mary, her poet-brother Rochford, and her poet-lover Wyatt. Happy would it have been for Anne Boleyn if parental ambition had never aimed at her fulfilling an higher destiny than becoming the wife of the accomplished and true-hearted Wyatt: that devoted friend, whose love, surviving the grave, lives still in the valuable biographical memorials which he preserved of her life.

Sir Thomas Wyatt died four years after the execution of Anne Boleyn; Percy only survived her a few months.

The motives for Anne's destruction were so glaringly unveiled by the indecorous and inhuman haste with which the king's marriage with Jane Seymour was celebrated, that a strong presumption of her innocence has naturally been the result with unprejudiced readers. André Thévet, a Franciscan, affirms, "that he was assured by several English gentlemen that Henry VIII., on his death-bed, expressed peculiar remorse for the wrong he had done Anne Boleyn by putting her to death on a false accusation." The Franciscans, as a body, had suffered so much for their steadfast support of the cause of queen Katharine, in opposition to the rival interests of queen Anne, that a testimony in favour of the latter, from one of that order, ought to be regarded as impartial history.

Anne Boleyn must have been in her thirty-sixth year at the time of her execution, for Cavendish tells us, that her brother, lord Rochford, was twenty-seven when he was appointed of the king's privy chamber. This was in 1527. The queen was probably about a year younger. This would have made her fourteen when she went to France as maid of honour to the bride of Louis XII., and thirty-two at the time of her acknowledged marriage with the king. She had been maid of honour to four queens, namely, Mary and Claude, queens of France, Margaret, queen of Navarre, and Katharine of Arragon, the first consort of Henry VIII., whom, in an evil hour for both, she supplanted in the affections of the king, and succeeded in her royal dignity as queen of England. She only survived the broken-hearted Katharine four months and a few days.

ELIZABETH I AND THE DEATH
OF MARY, QUEEN OF SCOTS

The unjust detention of Mary Queen of Scots in an English prison, had for fifteen years proved a source of personal misery to Elizabeth, and a perpetual incentive to crime. The worst passions of the human heart – jealousy, hatred, and revenge – were kept in a constant state of excitement by the confederacies that were formed in her dominions, in behalf of the captive heiress of the crown. Her ministers pursued a systematic course of espionage and treachery, in order to discover the friends of the unfortunate Mary; and when discovered, omitted no means, however base, by which they might be brought under the penalty of treason. The sacrifice of human life was appalling; the violation of all moral and divine restrictions of conscience more melancholy still. Scaffolds streamed with blood; the pestilential gaols were crowded with victims, the greater portion of whom died of fever or famine, unpitied and unrecorded, save in the annals of private families.

Mary Stuart was not only a king's daughter, but a crowned and anointed sovereign; and under no pretence, could she legally be rendered amenable to Elizabeth's authority. Every species of quiet cruelty that might tend to sap the life of a delicately-organized and sensitive female, had been systematically practised on the royal captive by the leaders of Elizabeth's cabinet. Mary had been confined in damp, dilapidated apartments, exposed to malaria, deprived of exercise and recreation, and compelled, occasionally, by way of variety, to rise from a sick bed, and travel through an inclement country, from one prison to another, in the depth of winter. These atrocities, had entailed upon her a complication of chronic maladies of the most agonizing description, but she continued to exist, and it was evident that the vital principle in her constitution, was sufficiently tenacious to enable her to endure many years of suffering. The contingencies of a day, an hour, meantime, might lay Elizabeth in the dust, and call Mary Stuart to the seat of empire. Could Burleigh, Walsingham, and Leicester expect, in that event, to escape the vengeance which their injurious treatment had provoked from that princess?

It is just possible, that Burleigh, rooted as he was to the helm of state, and skilled in every department of government, might, like Talleyrand, have made his defence good, and retained his office at court, if not his personal influence with the sovereign, under any change. He had observed an outward shew of civility to Mary, and was suspected, by Walsingham, of having entered into some secret pact with James of Scotland; but Walsingham and Leicester had committed themselves irrevocably, and, for them, there could be no other prospect than the block, if the Scottish queen, who was nine years younger than Elizabeth, outlived her.

From the moment that Elizabeth had declared that "honour and conscience both forbade her to put Mary to death," it had been the great business of these determined foes of Mary, to convince her that it was incompatible with her own safety, to permit her to live. Assertions to this effect, were lightly regarded by Elizabeth, but the evidence of a series of conspiracies, real as well as feigned, began to take effect upon her mind, and slowly, but surely, brought her to the same conclusion.

For many years it had been the practice of Walsingham to employ spies, not only for the purpose of watching the movements of those who were suspected of attachment to the Scottish queen, but to inveigle them into plots against the government and person of queen Elizabeth. One of these base agents, William Parry, after years of secret treachery in this abhorrent service, became himself a convert to the doctrines of the church of Rome, and conceived a design of assassinating queen Elizabeth. This he communicated to Neville, one of the English exiles, the claimant of the forfeit honours and estates of the last earl of Westmoreland. Neville, in the hope of propitiating the queen, gave prompt information of Parry's intentions against her majesty; but as Parry had formerly denounced Neville, Elizabeth, naturally imagining that he had been making a very bold attempt to draw Neville into an overt act of treason, directed Walsingham to inquire of the spy, whether he had recently, by way of experiment, suggested the idea of taking away her life to any one? If Parry had replied in the affirmative he would have been safe; but the earnest manner of his denial excited suspicion. He and Neville were confronted; and he then avowed "that he had felt so strong an impulse to murder the queen, that he had, of late, always left his dagger at home when summoned to her presence, lest he should fall upon her and slay her." This strange conflict of feeling appears like the reasoning madness of a monomaniac, and suggests the idea that Parry's mind had become affected with the delirious excitement of the times.

He was condemned to death, and on the scaffold cited his royal mistress to the tribunal of the all-seeing Judge, in whose presence he was about to appear.

The unhappy man expressly acquitted the queen of Scots of any knowledge of his designs. Mary herself, in her private letters, denies having the slightest connexion with him. The plot, however, furnished an excuse for treating her with greater cruelty than before. Her comparatively humane keeper, Sir Ralph Sadler, was superseded by Sir Amias Paulet and Sir Drue Drury, two rigid puritans, who were selected by Leicester for the ungracious office of embittering the brief and evil remnant of her days. The last report, made by Sadler, of the state of bodily suffering, to which the royal captive was reduced by her long and rigorous imprisonment, is very pitiable.

"I find her," says he, "much altered from what she was when I was first acquainted with her. She is not yet able to strain her left foot to the ground; and to her very great grief, not without tears, findeth it wasted and shrunk of its natural measure." In this deplorable state the hapless invalid was removed to the damp and dilapidated apartments of her former hated gaol, Tutbury Castle. A fresh access of illness was brought on by the inclemency of the situation, and the noxious quality of the air. She wrote a piteous appeal to Elizabeth, who did not vouchsafe a reply. Under these circumstances, the unfortunate captive caught, with feverish eagerness, at every visionary scheme that whispered to her in her doleful prison-house the flattering hope of escape. The zeal and self-devotion of her misjudging friends were the very means used by her foes to effect her destruction. Morgan, her agent in France, to whom allusion has already been made, was a fierce, wrong-headed Welchman, who had persuaded himself, and some others, that it was not only expedient but justifiable to destroy Elizabeth, as the sole means of rescuing his long-suffering mistress from the living death in which she was slowly pining away.

So greatly had Elizabeth's animosity against Morgan been excited, by the disclosures of Parry, that she declared "that she would give ten thousand pounds for his head." When she sent the order of the Garter to Henry III. she demanded that Morgan should be given up to her vengeance. Henry, who was doubtless aware that many disclosures might be forced from Morgan on the rack, that he would have the effect of committing himself with his good sister of England, endeavoured to satisfy her by sending Morgan to the Bastile, and forwarding his papers, or rather, it may be surmised, a discreet selection from them, to Elizabeth. But though the person of this restless intriguer was detained in prison, his friends were permitted to have access to him; and his plotting brain was employed in the organization of a more daring design against the life of queen Elizabeth that any that had yet been devised. Mary's faithful ambassador at Paris, Beaton, archbishop of Glasgow, and her kinsmen of the house of Guise, decidedly objected to the project.

Morgan, intent on schemes of vengeance, paid no heed to the remonstrances of Mary's tried and faithful counsellors, but took into his confidence two of Walsingham's most artful spies, in the disguise of Catholic priests – Gifford and Greatly by name – whom he recommended to the deluded Mary, as well as Poley and Maude, two other of the agents of that statesman. Easy enough would it have been for Walsingham, who had perfect information of the proceedings of the conspirators from the first, to have crushed the plot in its infancy; but it was his occult policy to nurse it till it became organized into a shape sufficiently formidable to Elizabeth, to bring her to the conclusion, that her life would never be safe while the Scottish queen was in existence, and, above all, to furnish a plausible pretext for the execution of Mary.

The principle leaders of the conspiracy were Ballard, a Catholic priest, and Savage, a soldier of fortune, who undertook to assassinate queen Elizabeth with his own hand. These unprincipled desperadoes, aided by their treacherous colleagues, succeeded in beguiling Anthony Babington of Dethick, a young gentleman of wealth and ancient lineage in Derbyshire, into the confederacy. Babington, who was a person of enthusiastic temperament, was warmly attached to the cause of Mary, for whom he had formerly performed the perilous service of transmitting letters during her imprisonment at Sheffield. At first, he objected to any attempt against his own sovereign; but the sophistry of Ballard, and the persuasions of the treacherous agents of Walsingham, not only prevailed over his scruples, but induced him to go the whole length of the plot, even to the proposed murder. This deed, he protested, ought not to be entrusted to the single arm of Savage, and proposed that six gentlemen should be associated for that purpose. How a man of a naturally generous and chivalric disposition could devise so cowardly a combination against the person of a female, appears almost incredible; but such was the blind excitement of party-feeling, and religious zeal, that he recklessly pressed onward to the accomplishment of his object, without even pausing to consider the turpitude of its design much less its absurdity. It is scarcely possible to imagine that Babington was a person of sound mind, when we find that he had his picture drawn with the six assassins grouped round him with the following Latin motto:

"Hi mihi sunt comites quos ipsa pericula jungunt:"
"My comrades these, whom very peril draws."

This picture, being shewn to Elizabeth, was probably instrumental in saving her life; for, soon after, while walking in Richmond Park, she observed a person loitering in her path, in whom she recognised the features of Barnwall, one of the leagued assassins, who had pledged themselves to take her life. Far from betraying the slightest feminine alarm, on this occasion, she fixed her eyes upon the lurking criminal, with a look that fairly daunted him, and turning to sir Christopher Hatton, and the other gentlemen in attendance, exclaimed, significantly, "Am I not well guarded today, not having one man, wearing a sword by his side, near me?" Barnwall afterwards deposed, that he distinctly heard the queen utter those words; on which, Sir Christopher Hatton told him, "that if others had observed him as closely as her majesty did, he had not escaped so easily."

Elizabeth, notwithstanding her intrepid deportment, on this occasion, liked not the predicament in which she stood, with an associated band of desperadoes at large, who had pledged themselves to take her life, and she was urgent for the apprehension of Ballard and Babington. Her wily ministers had, however, higher game to bring down than a few fanatic catholics. Walsingham had not wasted money and time, and woven his web with such determined subtlety, for the destruction of private individuals; his object was to entangle the queen of Scots into actual participation in a plot against Elizabeth's life and government. This had not yet been done, and he, with difficulty, prevailed on his royal mistress to allow matters to proceed for a few days longer. Elizabeth was, indeed, rather overborne, than persuaded, by her cabinet, on this occasion. Her feminine fears had been excited, and she said, "it was her duty to put an end to the evil designs of her enemies, while it was in her power to do so, lest, by not doing it, she should seem to tempt God's mercy, rather than manifest her trust in his protection." There was sound sense in this remark, and if her council had believed in the reality of her danger, they would have been without excuse, had they ventured to trifle with the safety of their sovereign for a single day.

At length, Mary was induced to write to the French and Spanish ambassadors, urging them to obtain from their respective courts, the assistance of men and money, to be employed in her deliverance.

Her letters were intercepted, opened, and copied, by Elizabeth's celebrated decipherer, Phillips, who was located under the same roof with the unsuspecting captive, at Chartley, together with Gregory, a noted seal-forger and opener of sealed letters. The labours of this worthy pair were not, it should appear, confined to opening and copying, verbatim, all the letters that were exchanged between Mary and her confederates.

Camden, the great contemporary historian, to whom Burleigh himself submitted all the *then* unbroken state-papers of Elizabeth's reign, assures us, that a postscript was added to one of Mary queen of Scots' letters to Babington, in the same characters used by her, containing an approval of the leading objects of the conspiracy.

The same day, letters to the Spanish ambassador, lord Paget, his brother Charles, the archbishop of

Glasgow, and Sir Francis Inglefield were intercepted.

The game was now considered, by Walsingham, sufficiently advanced for him to make a decided move, and he gave orders for the arrest of Ballard. Babington, almost immediately after this had been effected, encountered Savage, in one of the cloisters of old St. Paul's, and said to him, "Ballard is taken, and all will be betrayed. What remedy now?"

"None but to kill her presently," replied he.

"Then, go you to court, to-morrow," said Babington, "and execute the pact."

"Nay," replied Savage, "I cannot go to-morrow, my apparel is not ready, and in this apparel I shall never be allowed to come near the queen."

Babington gave him all the money he had about him, and his ring, and bade him to provide himself with what was needful, but Savage, like other bravoes, had boasted of that which he dared not attempt. He faltered – and neither he, nor either of the associate ruffians, would venture it.

Babington was at that time an invited guest, residing under Walsingham's own roof, and such was his infatuation, that he actually fancied he was the deceiver, instead of the dupe, of that most astute of all diplomatists, till one day, after the arrest of Ballard, a letter from the council, directing that he should be more closely watched, was brought to the under-secretary, Scudamore, who read it, incautiously, in his presence. A glance at the contents, which he contrived to read over Scudamore's shoulder, convinced him of his delusion, but dissembling his consternation, he effected his escape, the next night, from a tavern, where he was invited to sup, amidst the spies and servants of Walsingham. He gave the alarm to the other conspirators, and, having changed his beautiful complexion, by staining his face with walnut-skins, and cut off his hair, betook himself, with them, to the covert of St. John's Wood, near Marylebonne, which was at that time the formidable haunt of robbers and outlaws.

As soon as it was known that he had fled, warrants were issued for his apprehension, and very exaggerated accounts of the plot were published by Walsingham, stating "that a conspiracy to burn the city of London, and murder the queen, had been providentially discovered. That the combined forces of France and Spain had put to sea to invade England – that it was supposed they would effect a landing on the southern coast, and that all the papists were preparing to take up arms to join them." Such was the popular excitement at these frightful rumours, that all foreigners and catholics were in the greatest peril, and the ambassadors themselves were insulted and menaced in their own houses. When Babington and several of the conspirators were captured, and brought, under a strong guard, to the Tower, the most vehement satisfaction was expressed by the people, who followed them with shouts, singing psalms, and every demonstration of joy at the escape of the queen from their treasonable designs. The bells rang, bonfires were kindled, and every one appeared inspired with the most ardent loyalty towards their sovereign.

On the 13th of September, 1586, seven out of the fourteen conspirators were arraigned. They confessed their crime, and the depositions of Savage afford startling evidence, that the greatest danger to the person of the queen proceeded from the constant persuasions of Walsingham's spy, Gifford, for the deed to be attempted, at any time or place, where opportunity might serve. "As her majesty should go into her chapel to hear divine service," Gifford said, "he (Savage) might lurk in her gallery, and stab her with his dagger; or, if she should walk in her garden, he might shoot her with his dagg; or, if she should walk abroad to take the air, as she often did, accompanied rather with women than men, and those men slenderly weaponed, then might he assault her with his arming sword, and make sure work; and though he might hazard his own life, he would be sure to gain heaven thereby."

The greatest marvel in the whole business is, that such advice as this, addressed by Gifford in his feigned character of a Catholic priest, to men of weak judgments, excitable tempers, and fanatic principles, did not cost the queen her life. But Walsingham, in his insatiable thirst for the blood of Mary Stuart, appears to have forgotten that contingency, and even the possibility, that by employing agents to urge others to attempt the assassination of his sovereign, the accusation of devising her death might have been reported upon himself. Gifford was suffered to depart to France unquestioned and unmolested; but the fourteen deluded culprits were sentenced to expiate their guilt, by undergoing the dreadful penalty decreed by the law to traitors. Elizabeth was so greatly exasperated against them, that she intimated to her council the expediency of adopting "some new device," whereby their sufferings might be rendered more acute, and more calculated to strike terror into the spectators. Burleigh, with business-like coolness, explained to her majesty, "that the punishment prescribed by the letter of the law, was to the full as terrible as anything new that could be devised, if the executioner took care to protract the extremity of their pains in the sight of the multitude."

That functionary appears to have acted on this hint, by barbarously cutting the victims down before they were dead, and then proceeding to the completion of his horrible task on each in turn, according to the dread minutiæ of the sentence.

The revolting circumstances with which the executions of the seven principal conspirators were attended, excited the indignation of the by-standers to such a pitch, that her majesty found it expedient to issue an especial order, that the other seven should be more mercifully dealt with. They were therefore strangled, before the concluding horrors of the barbarous sentence were inflicted.

Immediately after the apprehension of Babington and his associates, Mary had been removed unexpectedly from Chartley to Tixal, and her papers and money seized during her absence. Her two secretaries, Nau and Curle, were arrested, and threatened with the rack, to induce them to bear witness against their unfortunate mistress. They were, at first, careful not to commit her by their admissions, which they well knew they could not do, without implicating themselves in the penalty. Burleigh, penetrating the motives of their reserve, wrote to Hatton his opinion, coupled with his facetious remark, "that they would yield somewhat to confirm their mistress' crimes, if they were persuaded that themselves might escape, and the blow fall upon their mistress between her head and her shoulders." This suggestion was acted upon, and combined with the terror, occasioned by the execution of Babington and his associates, drew from them sufficient admissions, to serve for evidence against their mistress.

The angry and excited state of feeling, to which Elizabeth's mind had been worked up, against her unfortunate kinswoman, may be plainly seen in the following letter, written by her to sir Amias Paulet, soon after the removal of the queen of Scots to the gloomy fortress of Fotheringaye.

QUEEN ELIZABETH TO SIR AMIAS PAULET

"Amias, my most faithful and careful servant, God reward thee treblefold for thy most troublesome charge so well discharged. If you knew, my Amias, how kindly, besides most dutifully, my grateful heart accepts and prizes your spotless endeavours and faultless actions, your wise orders and safe regard, performed in so dangerous and crafty a charge, it would ease your travails and rejoice your heart, in which I charge you place this most just thought, that I cannot balance in any weight of my judgment the value that I prize you at, and suppose no treasures to countervail such a faith. If I reward not such deserts, let me lack when I have most need of you; if I acknowledge not such merit, *non omnibus dictum.*

"Let your wicked murderess (*his prisoner, Mary queen of Scots*) know how, with hearty sorrow, her vile deserts compel these orders, and bid her, from me, ask God forgiveness for her treacherous dealings towards the saviour of her life many a year, to the intolerable peril of my own, and yet, not contented with so many forgiveness, must fault again so horribly, far passing woman's thought, much less a princess; instead of excusing whereof, not one can sorrow, it being so plainly confessed by the authors of my guiltless death.

"Let repentance take place, and let not the fiend possess her, so as her better part may not be lost, for which I pray with hands lifted up to Him, that may both save and spill.

"With my most loving adieu and prayer for thy long life, your most assured and loving sovereign, as thereby by good deserts induced."

The great point for which Burleigh, Leicester, Walsingham, and their colleagues, had been labouring for the last eighteen years, was, at length, accomplished. They had succeeded in persuading Elizabeth, that Mary Stuart, in her sternly-guarded prison, crippled with chronic and neuralgic maladies, surrounded by spies, and out of the reach of human aid, was so formidable to her person and government, that was an imperative duty to herself and her Protestant subjects to put her to death. Having once brought their long irresolute mistress to this conclusion, all other difficulties became matters of minor importance to the master spirits, who ruled Elizabeth's council, since they had only to arrange a ceremonial process for taking away the life of their defenceless captive, in as plausible and formal a manner as might be compatible with the circumstances of the case.

The commissioners for the trial of Mary, queen of Scots, left London for Fotheringaye Castle before the 8th of October, 1586; for, on that day, Davison dates a letter written to Burleigh, by her majesty's command, containing various instructions. In this letter, Davison informs the absent premier, that a Dutchman, newly arrived from Paris, who was familiar with the queen-mother's jeweller, had requested him to advise her majesty to beware of one who will present a petition to her on her way to chapel, or walking abroad. Davison goes on to request Burleigh to write to the queen, to pray her to be more circumspect of her person, and to avoid shewing herself in public, till the brunt of the business then in hand be overblown.

This mysterious hint of a new plot against the queen's life was in conformity with the policy of the cabinet, which referred all attempts of the kind to the evil influence of the captive, Mary Stuart. From the same letter we learn, that Elizabeth had directed her lord-chamberlain to give a verbal answer to the remonstrance of the French ambassador against bringing the queen of Scots to a trial, and that the answer expressed her resentment at his presumption in attempting to school her. In conclusion, Davison informs Burleigh and Walsingham, that he is especially commanded by her majesty to signify to them both "how greatly she doth long to hear how her *Spirit* and her *Moon* do find themselves, after so foul and wearisome a journey." By the above pet names was the mighty Elizabeth accustomed, in moments of playfulness, to designate those grave and unbending statesmen, Burleigh and Walsingham; but playfulness at such a season was certainly not only in bad taste, but revolting to every feeling of humanity, when the object of that foul and weary journey, on which Elizabeth's Spirit and her Moon had departed, is considered.

The most repulsive feature, in the final proceedings against the hapless Mary, is the odious levity with which the leading actors in the tragedy demeaned themselves, while preparing to shed her blood, and, at the same time, appealing to the Scriptures in justification of the deed. L'Aubespine de Chasteauneuf, the French ambassador, demanded, in the name of his sovereign, that Mary might be allowed the assistance of counsel. Elizabeth returned an angry verbal answer by Hatton, that "she required not the advice or schooling of foreign powers to instruct her how she ought to act;" and added, "that she considered the Scottish queen unworthy of counsel."

What, it may be asked, was this but condemnation before trial? and what result was to be expected from the trial of any person of whom a despotic sovereign had made such an assertion? Can any one read Elizabeth's letter to the commissioners, dated October 7th, in which she charges them "to forbear passing sentence on the Scottish queen till they have returned into her presence, and made their report to herself," and doubt that the death of the royal captive was predetermined? It was not till the 11th, four days after the date of this letter, that they assembled at Fotheringaye for the business on which they had been deputed. On the 12th, they opened their court. Mary refused to acknowledge their authority, on which they delivered to her the following letter from their royal mistress:

QUEEN ELIZABETH
TO MARY QUEEN OF SCOTS.

"You have, in various ways and manners, attempted to take my life, and to bring my kingdom to destruction by bloodshed. I have never proceeded so harshly against you, but have, on the contrary, protected and maintained you like myself. These treasons will be proved to you, and all made manifest.

"Yet it is my will that you answer the nobles and peers of the kingdom as if I were myself present. I, therefore, require, charge, and command, that you make answer, for I have been well informed of your arrogance.

"Act plainly, without reserve, and you will sooner be able to obtain favour of me."

"ELIZABETH."

This letter, was addressed to Mary, (without the superscription of cousin or sister,) and as it may be supposed, from the well-known high spirit of that queen, had not the slightest effect in inducing her to reply to the commissioners. She told them, however, "that she had endeavoured to gain her liberty, and would continue to do so as long as she lived; but that she had never plotted against the life of their queen, nor had any connexion with Babington or the others, but to obtain her freedom; on which particulars, if Elizabeth chose to question her in person, she would declare the truth, but would reply to no inferior." There was no little sagacity shewn in this appeal of Mary to the inquisitiveness that formed a leading trait of Elizabeth's character.

After two days fruitless struggle to defend herself against the subtlety and oppression of men, who demeaned themselves like adverse lawyers pleading on the side of the crown rather than as conscientious judges, Mary demanded to be heard before the assembled parliament of England, or the queen and her council. The commissioners then adjourned the court, to meet, October 25th, at the Star Chamber, Westminster. On that day they reassembled, and pronounced sentence of death on the Scottish queen, pursuant to the statute of the 27th of Elizabeth, which had been framed for that very purpose.

The parliament met on the 29th, and, having considered the reports of the commissioners, united in petitioning queen Elizabeth that the sentence against the Scottish queen might be carried into execution. Elizabeth received the deputation from parliament, November 12th, in her presence-chamber at Richmond palace. Mr. Sergeant Puckering, the speaker, after enlarging on the offences of Mary against queen Elizabeth, recalled to her majesty the example of God's displeasure on Saul for sparing Agag, and on Ahab for preserving Benhadad; and, after preaching a political sermon, he assured her, "that her compliance with the petition would be most acceptable to God, and that her people expected nothing less of her."

The parliament responded, in the tone that was desired, with a more ardent requisition for the blood of Mary. Elizabeth faltered – not from womanly feelings of tenderness and compassion towards the defenceless object of their fury, but from certain doubts and misgivings within her own mind, which produced one of her characteristic fits of irresolution. Her mind was tempest-tossed between her desire of Mary's death, and her reluctance to stand forth to the world as her acknowledged executioner. She would have the deed performed "some other way." But how?

One, at least, of her ministers entered into the feelings of his royal mistress on this delicate subject, and to his eternal infamy, endeavoured to relieve her from her embarrassment, as to the means of removing the victim, without the undesirable *éclat* of a public execution. Leicester wrote from Holland to suggest "the sure but silent operation of poison." He even sent a divine over to convince the more scrupulous Walsingham of the lawfulness of the means proposed; but that stern politician was resolutely bent on maintaining a show of justice, and at the same time, exalting the power of his royal mistress, by bringing the queen of Scotland to the block. Burleigh coincided in this determination, and in his letters to Leicester complained, "that the queen's slackness, did not stand with her surety or their own." The personal influence of Leicester with the sovereign, appears to have been required for the consummation of the tragedy. He was remanded home in November, and seems to have taken an active part in preventing Elizabeth from swerving from the point to which her ministers had brought her.

On the 22nd of November, lord Buckhurst and sir Robert Beale, proceeded, in pursuance of the orders in council, and her majesty's commands, to Fortheringaye Castle, to announce to the queen of

Scots, that sentence of death had been pronounced against her by the commissioners, and ratified by the parliament of England. They executed their ungracious errand without the slightest delicacy or consideration for the feelings of the royal victim, telling her, "that she must not hope for mercy," adding taunts on the score of her religious opinions, very much at variance with the divine spirit of Christianity, and concluded by ordering her chamber and her bed to be hung with black. The conduct of sir Amias Paulet, was even more gratuitously brutal and unmanly, and reflects great disgrace on the character of any sovereign to whom such petty instances of malice could be supposed acceptable proofs of his zeal against her fallen enemy.

Meantime, the French ambassador L'Aubespine Chateauneuf, having written in great alarm to Henry III., that the queen of England was proceeding, he feared, to extremities with the queen of Scots, and urged him to interfere for her preservation, that monarch despatched M. de Pomponne de Bellievre, as an ambassador-extraordinary, for the purpose of remonstrating with Elizabeth against the outrage she was preparing to commit, and using every species of intercession for the preservation of Mary's life.

Bellievre landed at Dover, after a stormy passage, November 29th, having suffered so severely from sea-sickness, together with one of the gentlemen of the suite, that they were unable to proceed till they had reposed themselves for a day and night. Elizabeth, or her council, more probably, took advantage of this circumstance to delay the new envoy's audience, under pretence, that he and his company had brought the infection of the plague from France, and that it would be attended with great peril to her royal person if she admitted them into her presence.

It was also asserted, that Bellievre had brought over some unknown men, who had come expressly to assassinate her. These reports appear to have been very offensive to the embassy, and are ascribed by the indignant secretary of legation, by whom the transactions of that eventful period, were recorded for the information of his own court, "to the infinite malice of the queen."

Elizabeth had withdrawn to her winter quarters at Richmond, and it was not till the 7th of December, that the urgency of Bellievre induced her to grant him his first audience. He came to her after dinner on that day, accompanied by L'Aubespine, the resident French minister, and all the gentlemen who had attended him from France. Elizabeth received them in her presence-chamber, seated on her throne, and surrounded by her nobles and the lords of her council. Leicester had placed himself in close contiguity to the royal person; but when the French envoy proceeded to open the business on which he came, she bade her presumptuous master of the horse, "fall back." His colleagues hearing this command addressed to him, took the hint, and withdrew also, to a little distance. Bellievre then delivered the remonstrances on the part of his sovereign, in behalf of the Scottish queen, his sister-in-law. Elizabeth interrupted him many times, answering him point by point, speaking in good French, but so loud, that she could be heard all over the saloon. When she mentioned the queen of Scots, she appeared under the influence of passion, which was expressed by her countenance. She burst into invectives against her, accused her of ingratitude for the many favours which she said "she had conferred upon her;" although it was impossible for hatred and revenge to have worked more deadly mischief against another, than such love as hers had wrought to the hapless victim of her treachery. She went on to comment on the address Bellievre had just delivered, observing, "that monseigneur had quoted several examples drawn from history; but she had read much and seen many books in her lifetime, – more, indeed, than thousands of her sex and rank had done; but never had she met with, or heard of, such an attempt as that which had been planned against her by her own kinswoman, whom the king her brother-in-law ought not to support in her malice, but rather to aid her in bringing speedily to justice."

Elizabeth went on to say, "that she had had great experience in the world, having known what it was to be both subject and sovereign, and the difference also between good neighbours and those who were evilly disposed towards her. She told Bellievre, who was a nobleman of high rank and singular eloquence, "that she was very sorry he had not been sent on a better occasion; that she had been compelled to come to the resolution she had taken, because it was impossible to save her own life if she preserved the queen of Scots; but if the ambassadors could point out any means whereby she might do it, consistently with her own security, she should be greatly obliged to them, never having shed so many tears at the death of her father, of her brother king Edward, or her sister Mary, as she had done for this unfortunate affair."

Rapin, with sophistry unworthy of a historian, says – "The queen of Scots and her friends had brought matters to such a pass, that one of the queens must perish, and it was natural that the weakest should fall." This was decidedly untrue. The royal authority of Elizabeth was never more firmly established than at this very period. She could have nothing to apprehend from the sick, helpless, and impoverished captive at Fotheringaye. It was to the ministers of Elizabeth and their party, that Mary was an object of alarm; consequently, it was their interest to keep the mind of their royal mistress in a constant state of excitement, by plots and rumours of plots, till they had wrought her irritable temper up to the proper pitch. Among the many means resorted to for that purpose by Burleigh, may, in all probability, be reckoned the celebrated letter, which has been published, in Murdin's State Papers, as the production of Mary queen of Scots, in whose name it was written, but which bears every mark of the grossest forgery. It is written in French, and details, with provoking minuteness, a variety of scandals, which appear to have been in circulation against queen Elizabeth in her own court. These are affirmed to have been repeated to the captive queen by the countess of Shrewbury, who, during the life of her first husband, Mr. Saintlow, was one of Elizabeth's bed-chamber women. Lady Shrewsbury was a malignant gossip and intriguante, and on very ill terms with her husband's royal charge. These circumstances give some plausibility to the idea that Mary wrote this letter, in order to destroy her great enemy's credit with the queen.

Mary had made, at various times, very serious complaints of the insolence of this vulgar-minded woman, and of the aspersions which she had cast on her own character; and she had also requested the French ambassador to inform the queen Elizabeth of her treasonable intrigues in favour of her little grand-daughter, lady Arabella Stuart; but that Mary ever departed so far from the character of a gentlewoman, as to commit to paper the things contained in this document, no one who is familiar with the pure and delicate style which forms the prevailing charm of her authentic letters can believe. Neither was Mary so deplorably ignorant of the human heart, as not to be aware that the person who has so little courtesy as to repeat to another painful and degrading reports, becomes invariably an object of greater dislike to that person than the originator of the scandal.

Every sentence of the letter has been artfully devised, for the express purpose of irritating Elizabeth, not only against lady Shrewbury, but against Mary herself, who would never have had the folly to inform her jealous rival, "that lady Shrewsbury had, by a book of divination in her possession, predicted that Elizabeth would very soon be cut off by a violent death, and Mary would succeed to her throne." What was this but furnishing Elizabeth with a cogent reason for putting her to death without further delay? The letter, as a whole, will not bear insertion; it contains very offensive observations on Elizabeth's person, constitution, and conduct, which are there affirmed to have been made by lady Shrewsbury, together with a repetition of much indelicate gossip, touching her majesty's intimacy with Simier, the plenipotentiary of Francis duke of Anjou, with Anjou himself, and with Hatton; but strange to say, not a word about Leicester, which is the more worthy of remark, inasmuch as the scandals respecting Elizabeth and Leicester had been very notorious, however devoid of foundation they might have been in point of fact.

Leicester was justly regarded by Mary queen of Scots, as one of her greatest enemies. He is always mentioned with peculiar bitterness in her letters to her friends, and if the celebrated scandal letter, in Murdin, had really been written by her, she would scarcely have omitted having a fling at him. Instead of this, the great stress is laid against Leicester's personal rival, Hatton, who is provokingly stated "to have been, at times, so thoroughly ashamed of the public demonstrations of her majesty's fondness, that he was constrained to retire." Some allusion is also made to a love-quarrel between Elizabeth and Hatton, about certain gold buttons on his dress, on which occasion he departed out of her presence, in a fit of choler; that she sent Killigrew after him, in great haste, and bestowed a buffet on her messenger when he came back without him, and that she pensioned another gentleman, with three hundred a year, for bringing her news of Hatton's return; that when she said Hatton might have contracted an illustrious marriage, he dared not, for fear of offending her; and, for the same cause, the earl of Oxford was afraid of appearing on good terms with his wife; that lady Shrewsbury had advised her, (the queen of Scots,) laughing excessively at the same time, to place her son in the list of her majesty's lovers, for she was so vain, and had so high an opinion of her own beauty, that she fancied herself into some heavenly goddess, and, if she took it into her head, might easily be persuaded to entertain the youthful king of Scots as one of her suitors; that no flattery was too absurd for her to receive, for those about her were accustomed to tell her, "that they could not look full upon her, because her face was as resplendent as the sun;" and that the countess of Shrewsbury declared, "that she

117

and lady Lenox never dared look at each other, for fear of bursting out a laughing, when in Elizabeth's presence, because of her affection," adding, "that nothing in the world would induce her daughter, Talbot, to hold any office near her majesty's person, for fear she should, in one of her furies, treat her as she had done her cousin Scudamore, whose finger she had broken, and then tried to make her courtiers believe that it was done by the fall of a chandelier; that she had cut another of her attendants across the hand with a knife, and that her ladies were accustomed to mimic and take the queen off, for the amusement of their waiting women; and, above all, that lady Shrewsbury had asserted, "that the queen's last illness proceeded from an attempt to heal the disease in her leg," with many other remarks equally vexatious.

If Elizabeth really believed this letter to have been written by Mary, it is impossible to wonder at the animosity she evinced against her, since the details it contained were such as few women could forgive another for repeating.

The young king of Scotland addressed a letter, of earnest and indignant remonstrance, to Elizabeth, on the subject of his unfortunate mother, and directed sir William Keith, his ambassador, to unite with the French ambassador in all the efforts he made for averting the doom that was now impending over her. Elizabeth long delayed an audience to Keith, and when she did admit him to her presence, she behaved with her wonted duplicity. "I swear, by the living God," said she, "that I would give one of my own arms to be cut off so that any means could be found for us both to live in assurance." In another interview, she declared, "that no human power should ever persuade her to sign the warrant for Mary's execution." When, however, James was informed that the sentence against his mother had been published, he wrote a letter expressed in menacing and passionate terms. Elizabeth broke into a storm of fury when Keith delivered his remonstrances, and was with difficulty prevented from driving him from her presence. Leicester, it appears, interposed, and at last succeeded in pacifying her, and inducing her, on the following day, to dictate a more moderate reply. Unfortunately, James also abated his lofty tone, and wrote an apology to his royal godmother. From that moment, Elizabeth, knew that the game was in her own hands, and bore herself with surpassing insolence to the Scotch envoys, who were sent to expostulate with her by James.

The particulars of her reception of the proposals communicated to her, in the name of king James, by the master of Gray, are preserved in a memorial drawn up by himself. "No one," he says, "was sent to welcome and conduct him into the presence of the queen, and it was ten days before he and his coadjutor, sir Robert Melvil, were admitted to an audience." Now, although this uncourteous delay proceeded from herself, Elizabeth's first address was in those blunt terms:"A thing long looked for should be welcome when it comes; I would now see your master's orders."

Gray desired, first, to be assured that the cause for which they were to be made, was "still *extant*." Meaning that it was reported that the Scottish queen had been already put to death. "I think," said Elizabeth, coolly, "it be extant yet, but I will not promise for an hour."

She rejected the conditions they offered, in the name of the king their master, with contempt, and calling in Leicester, the lord-admiral, and Hatton, very despitefully repeated them in the hearing of them all. Gray then proposed that Mary should demit her right of succession to the crown of England, in favour of her son, by which means the hopes of the catholics would be cut off. Elizabeth pretended not to understand the import of this proposition; on which Leicester explained, that it simply meant, that the king of Scots should be put in his mother's place, as successor to the crown of England.

"Is it so?" exclaimed Elizabeth, with a loud voice, and terrible oath, "get rid of one and have a worse in her place? Nay, then, I put myself in a worse place than before. By God's passion! that were to cut my own throat! and for a duchy or earldom to yourself, you, or such as you, would cause some of your desperate knaves to kill me." This gracious observation appears to have been aimed at Leicester, to mark her displeasure at his interference in attempting to explain that which it was not her wish to understand, in allusion to the delicate point of the succession; and it is more than probable that she suspected that the proposition was merely a lure, concerted between Gray and Leicester, to betray her into acknowledging the king of Scots as her successor.

"No, by God!" concluded she, "he shall never be in that place," and prepared to depart. Gray solicited that Mary's life might be spared for fifteen days, to give them time to communicate with the king their master, but she peremptorily refused. Melvil implored for only eight days, "No," exclaimed Elizabeth, rising from her seat, "not for an hour!" and so left them.

The expostulations of Melvil in behalf of his royal mistress, were as sincere as they were manly and courageous, but the perfidious Gray secretly persuaded Elizabeth to slay, and not spare, by whispering in her ear, the murderous proverb, "*Mortua non mordet*," – "a dead woman bites not."

The state of Elizabeth's mind, just before she was induced to sign the death-warrant, is thus described by the graphic pen of the contemporary historian, Camden: "In the midst of those doubtful and perplexing thoughts, that she gave herself over to solitariness, she sate many times melancholy and mute, and frequently sighing, muttered this to herself, '*aut fer, aut feri,*' that is, either bear with her or smite her; and '*ne feriare feri,*' – 'strike, lest thou be stricken.' At this period she was also heard to lament, 'that among the thousands who professed to be attached to her as a sovereign, not one would spare her the painful task of dipping her hands in the blood of a sister queen."

The idea of ridding herself of her royal prisoner by a private murder, the usual fate of captive princes, appears to have taken a powerful hold of Elizabeth's mind, during the last eight days of Mary's life. In fact, the official statements of Mr. Secretary Davison, afford positive proof that she had provided herself with agents, one of whom, Wingfield, she named, "who were ready," she said, "to undertake the deed." The "niceness" of those "precise fellows," Paulet and Drury, who had the custody of Mary's person, frustrated Elizabeth's project; they were too scrupulous or too cautious to become accomplices in the murder of their hapless charge, in any other way than by assisting at her execution, authorized by the queen's own warrant, under the royal seal. They were aware of the guerdon, generally assigned to those, who lend themselves to perform the unprofitable works of darkness for their betters. History had not told the tale of Gournay and Maltravers, and other tools of royal villainy in vain to the shrewd castellans of Fotheringaye castle; and the subsequent treatment of Davison, demonstrated their wisdom in refusing to implicate themselves in an iniquity, so full of peril to inferior agents.

The particulars of this foul passage, in the personal annals of the maiden queen, shall be related by Davison himself.

"After that the sentence against the Scottish queen was passed, and subscribed by the lords and others, the commissioners appointed to her trial, and that her majesty had notified the same to the world by her proclamation, according to the statute, there remained nothing but her warrant, under the great seal of England, for the performing and accomplishing her execution, which, after some instance, as well of the lords and commons, of the whole parliament then assembled, as of others of her council, and best affected subjects, it pleased her majesty at length to yield thereunto; and thereupon gave order to my lord-treasurer to project the same, which he accordingly performed, and with her majesty's privity, left in my hands, to procure her signature; but by reason of the presence of the French and Scotch ambassadors, then suitors for her (Mary's) life, she (queen Elizabeth) forbore the signing thereof, till the first of February, which was some days after their departure home. At what time her majesty, after some conference with the lord-admiral, of the great danger she constantly lived in, and moved by his lordship to have more regard to the surety of herself and state, than she seemed to take, resolved to defer the said execution no longer, and gave orders to his lordship to send for me, to bring the warrant unto her to be signed, which he, forthwith, did, by a messenger of the chamber, who found me in the park, whither I had newly gone to take the air; whereupon returning back immediately with him, I went directly up to the privy-chamber, where his lordship, attending my coming, discoursed unto me what speech had passed that morning betwixt her majesty and him, touching the justice against the said Scottish queen, and finally told me, "how she was now fully resolved to proceed to the accomplishment thereof, and had commanded him to send expressly for me, to bring the warrant unto her to be signed, that it might be forthwith despatched, and deferred no longer." According to which direction, I went immediately to my chamber, to fetch the said warrant, and other things touching her service, and returning up again, I sent in Mrs. Brooke, to signify my being there to her majesty, who presently called for me.

"At my coming in, her highness first demanded of me, – 'Whether I had been abroad that fair morning?' advising me 'to use it oftener,' and reprehending me 'for the neglect thereof,' with other like gracious speeches, arguing care of my health, and finally asked me, 'What I had in my hands?' I answered, 'Divers things to be signed that concerned her service.' She inquired, 'Whether my lord-admiral had not given me order to bring up the warrant for the Scottish queen's execution?' I answered, 'Yes;' and thereupon asking me for it, I delivered it into her hands. After the reading whereof, she, calling for pen and ink, signed it, and laying it from her on the mats, demanded of me, 'Whether I were not heartily sorry to see it done?' My answer was, 'that I was so far from taking pleasure in the calamity or fall of any, or, otherwise, from thirsting in any sort after the blood of this unhappy lady in particular, as I could not but be heartily grieved to think that one of her place and quality, and otherwise so near unto her majesty, should give so great cause as she had done to take this resolution; but seeing the life of that queen threatened her majesty's death, and therefore this act of hers, in all men's opinions, was of that justice and necessity, that she could not defer it without the manifest wrong and danger of herself and the whole realm, I could not be sorry to see her take an honourable and just course of securing the one and the other, as he that preferred the death of the guilty before the innocent;' which answer her highness approving with a smiling countenance, passed from the matter to ask me, 'What else I had to sign?' and thereupon offering unto her some other warrants and instructions touching her service, it pleased her, with the best disposition and willingness that might be, to sign and dispatch them all."

"After this, she commanded me to carry it to the seal, and to give my lord-chancellor special order to use it as secretly as might be, lest the divulging thereof before the execution might, as she pretended, increase her danger; and in my way to my lord-chancellor, her pleasure also was, that I should visit Mr. Secretary Walsingham, being then sick at his home in London, and communicate the matter to him, 'because the grief thereof would go near,' as she merrily said, 'to kill him outright;' then taking occasion to repeat unto me some reasons why she had deferred the matter so long, as, namely, 'for her honour's sake that the world might see that she had not been violently or maliciously drawn thereto.'"

How these professions agreed with her majesty's merry message to Walsingham, apprising him that she had just signed the fatal instrument for shedding the blood of her nearest relative, by the axe of the executioner, the unprejudiced reader may judge. Little, indeed, did Elizabeth, in the full confidence of her despotic power, imagine that the dark import of her secret communings with her secretary in that private closet, would one day be proclaimed to the whole world, by the publication of the documentary evidences of her proceedings. When the Ithuriel spear of truth withdraws the curtain from scenes like these, the reverse of the picture suddenly unveiled to those who have been taught, even in the nursery, to revere in "good queen Bess" the impersonification of all that is great and glorious in woman, is startling.

"The queen concluded," continues Davison, "that she never was so ill-advised as not to apprehend her own danger, and the necessity she had to proceed to this execution; and thereupon, after some intermingled speech to and fro, told me that she would have it done as secretly as might be, appointing the hall where she (queen Mary) was, for the place of execution, and misliking the court, or green of the castle, for divers respects, she alleged, with other speech to like effect. Howbeit, as I was ready to depart, she fell into some complaint of sir Amias Paulet and others, 'that might have eased her of this burden,' wishing that Mr. Secretary (Walsingham) and I would yet to write unto both him and sir Drue Drury, to sound their disposition in this behalf.

"And," continues Davison, "albeit, I had before excused myself from meddling therein, upon sundry her majesty's former motions, as a matter I utterly prejudged, assuring her, 'that it would be so much labour lost, knowing the wisdom and integrity of the gentlemen, whom I thought would not do so unlawful an act for any respect in the world;' yet, finding her desirous to have the matter attempted, I promised, for her satisfying, to signify this her pleasure to Mr. Secretary, and so, for that time leaving her, went down directly to my lord-treasurer, (Burleigh,) to whom I did communicate the said warrant signed, together with such other particulars as had passed at that time between her highness and me. The same afternoon I waited on my lord-chancellor for the sealing of the said warrant, according to her majesty's direction, which was done between the hours of four and five, from whence I returned back unto Mr. Secretary Walsingham, whom I had visited by the way, and acquainted with her pleasure, touching the letters that were to be written to the said sir Amias Paulet and sir Drue Drury, which, at my return, I found ready to be sent away."

The reader is here presented with the copy of the private official letter, in which the two secretaries propose the murder, in plain and direct terms, to Paulet and Drury, by the express commands of their royal mistress:

WALSINGHAM AND DAVISON TO SIR AMIAS PAULET AND SIR DRUE DRURY.

"February 1, 1586–7.

"After our hearty commendations, we find, by a speech lately made by her majesty (queen Elizabeth), that she doth note in you both, a lack of that care and zeal for her service, that she looketh for at your hands, in that you have not, in all this time, (of yourselves, without other provocation,) found out some way of *shortening the life of the Scots' queen*, considering the great peril she (queen Elizabeth) is hourly

subject to, *so long as the said queen shall live*;
wherein, besides a kind of lack of love towards
her, she wonders greatly that you have not that
care of your own particular safeties, or rather
the preservation of religion and the public
good, and prosperity of your country, that
reason and policy commandeth, especially
having so good a warrant and ground for the
satisfaction of your consciences towards God,
and the discharge of your credit and reputation
towards the world, as the oath of association,
which you have both so solemnly taken and
vowed, especially the matter wherewith *she*
(Mary) standeth charged, being so clearly and
manifestly proved against her.

"And, therefore, *she* (Elizabeth) taketh it
most unkindly, that men, professing that love
towards her that you do, should, in a kind of
sort, for lack of discharging your duties, cast
the burden upon her, knowing, as you do,
her indisposition to shed blood, especially of
one of that sex and quality, and so near her in
blood, as that queen is.

"These respects, we find, do greatly trouble
her majesty, who, we assure you, hath sundry
times protested, 'that if the regard of the danger
of her good subjects and faithful servants, did

not more move her than her own peril, she would never be drawn to the shedding of blood.'

"We thought it meet to acquaint you with these speeches, lately passed from her majesty, referring the same to your good judgments. And so we commit you to the protection of the Almighty.

"Your most assured friends,
"FRA. WALSINGHAM.
"WILL. DAVISON."

An anonymous writer, whose work was published before the learned research of Hearne had drawn this disgraceful document, and the reply of the uncompromising castellans of Fotheringaye, from the dust and darkness in which the correspondence had slumbered for upward of two centuries, possessed traditional evidence of the fact, that a letter was sent, by the queen's command, to instigate sir Amias Paulet to the assassination of his hapless charge. It was scarcely possible that he should be aware that the veritable letter was absolutely extant; and, as he adds, a remarkable incident, illustrative of the excited state of Elizabeth's mind, the night after it had been dispatched, the passage is well worthy of quotation.

"Some say," observes our author, "she sent orders to Paulet to make away with the queen of Scots; but in the midst of that very night she was awakened by a violent shriek from the lady who always slept in her bed-chamber. The queen asked her 'what ailed her?' She answered, 'I dreamed that I saw the hangman strike off the head of the queen of Scots; and forthwith he laid hands on your majesty, and was to behead you as well, when I screamed with terror.'

"The queen exclaimed, 'I was, at the instant you awoke me, dreaming the very same dream.'"

It is curious enough, that this wild story of Elizabeth's midnight vision is confirmed by her own words, quoted in Davison's autograph narrative, to which we will now return.

After stating that the morning after the precious scroll to Paulet and Drury had been despatched, Killigrew came to him, with a message from the queen, importing 'that if he had not been to the lord-chancellor, he should forbear going to him till he had spoke again with her;' which message coming too late, he proceeded to her majesty, to give an account of what he had done. He thus continues – "At my coming to her, she demanded of me, 'Whether the warrant were passed the seal?' I told her, 'Yes.' She asked, 'What needeth that

haste?' I answered, 'That I had therein made no
more haste than herself commanded, and my duty,
in a case of that moment, required, which, as I took
it, was not to be dallied with.' 'But methinketh,'
said she, 'that it might have been otherwise handled,
for the form,' naming into me some that were of
that opinion, whose judgments she commended.
I answered, 'that I took the honourable and just
way, to be the safest and best way, if they meant to
have it done at all;' whereto her majesty replying
nothing, for that time, left me, and went to dinner.
From her, I went to Mr. Vice-chamberlain Hatton,
with whom I did communicate the warrant and
other particulars that had passed between her
highness and me, touching the despatch thereof,
when, falling into a rehearsal of some doubtful
speeches of hers, betraying a disposition to throw
the burden from herself, if by any means she
might, and remembering unto him the example
of her dealing in the case of the duke of Norfolk's
execution, which she had laid heavily upon my
lord-treasurer, (Burleigh,) for a long time after, and
how much more her disavowing this justice was
to be feared, considering the timorousness of her
sex and nature, the quality of the person whom it
concerned, and respect of her friends, with many
other circumstances that might further incline

her thereunto, I finally told him, 'that I was, for mine own part, fully resolved, notwithstanding the directions I had received to do nothing that might give her any advantage to cast a burden of so great weight upon my single and weak shoulders, and, therefore, having done as much as belonged to my part, would leave to him and others as deeply interested in the surety of her majesty and the state, as myself, to advise what course should now be taken for accomplishing the rest."

Hatton's rejoinder to these observations was, "that he was heartily glad the matter was brought thus far, and, for his part, 'he would wish him hanged who would not cooperate in a cause, which so much concerned the safety of the queen and her realm.'" On further consultation, they both decided on going to Burleigh, with whom they agreed that the matter should be communicated to the rest of the lords of the council, and Burleigh took upon himself to prepare the letters to the earls of Shrewsbury and Kent, and the others to whom the warrant was directed. The next morning, Burleigh sent for Davison and Hatton, and shewed the draught he had drawn up of those letters. Hatton considered them too particular in the wording, on which Burleigh offered to draw up others, in more general terms, against the afternoon. The council, being apprised of the business in hand, met in Burleigh's chamber where he, entering into the particulars of the Scottish queen's offence, the danger of her majesty and state, and the necessity of this execution, and, having shewn them the warrant, he apprised them of the suspected intention of the sovereign to shift the burden of it from herself, if she could. It is probable, too, that Elizabeth's earnest desire of having the deed performed by a private murder, which she would afterwards charge on whomsoever she could induce to undertake it, was also discussed, but, at all events, the council came to the unanimous resolution, that the warrant should be forthwith despatched, without troubling her majesty any more about it. The subtle conclave, who thus presumed to secure themselves, by outwitting their sovereign, and acting independently of her commands, did Beale (the clerk of the council) the honour of considering him the fittest person to whom they could commit the charge of putting the warrant for the death of the rightful heiress of the throne into execution. He accepted the office, and approved the copies of the letters devised by Burleigh, and having appointed them to be written out fair, against the afternoon, they went to dinner, and, between one and two o'clock, returned to have the letters signed, that were addressed to the lords and commissioners, appointed to that duty. These were then delivered to Beale, with earnest request for him to use the utmost diligence in expediting the same.

Elizabeth, meantime, unconscious of the proceedings of her ministers, was still brooding vainly over the idea of a private murder. "The next morning," pursues Davison, "her majesty being in some speech with Burleigh, in the private chamber, seeing me come in, called me to her, and, as if she had understood nothing of these proceedings, smiling, told me, 'she had been troubled that night upon a dream she had, that the Scottish queen was executed,' pretending to have been so greatly moved, with the news, against me, as in that passion she would have done I wot not what." But this being in a pleasant and smiling manner, I answered her majesty, 'that it was good for me I was not near her, so long as that humour lasted.' But withal, taking hold of her speech, asked her, in great earnest, 'what it meant? and whether, having proceeded thus far, she had not a full and resolute meaning to go through with the said execution, according to the warrant?' Her answer was, 'Yes,' confirmed with a solemn oath, 'only that she thought that it might have received a better form, because this threw all the responsibility upon her herself.' I replied, 'that the form prescribed by the warrant was such as the law required, and could not well be altered, with any honesty, justice, or surety to those who were commissioners therein; neither did I know who could sustain this burthen, if she took it not upon her, being sovereign magistrate, to whom the sword was committed, of God, for the punishment of the wicked, and defence of the good, and without whose authority, the life or member of the poorest wretch in her kingdom could not be touched.'"

"She answered, 'that there were wiser men than myself in the kingdom, of other opinion.' I told her, 'I could not answer for other men, yet, this I was sure of, that I had never yet heard any man give a sound reason to prove it either honourable or safe for her majesty, to take any other course than that which standeth with law and justice;' and so, without further replication or speech, we parted.

"The same afternoon, (as I take it,) she asked me, 'Whether I had heard from sir Amias Paulet?' I told her, 'No;' but within an hour after, going to London, I met, with letters from him, in answer to those that were written unto him, some few days before, upon her commandment."

This portion of the narrative would be incomplete without the insertion of these memorable letters:

SIR AMIAS PAULET
TO SECRETARY WALSINGHAM.

"SIR, – Your letters of yesterday coming to my hands this present day, at five post meridian, I would not fail, according to your direction, to return my answer, with all possible speed, which I shall deliver to you with great grief and bitterness of mind, in that I am so unhappy as living to see this unhappy day, in which I am required, by direction from my most gracious sovereign, to do an act which God and the law forbiddeth.

"My goods and my life are at my majesty's *disposition* (disposal), and I am ready to lose them the next morrow if it shall please her, acknowledging that I do not hold them as of her mere and most gracious favour, and do not desire to enjoy them, but with her highness' good liking. But God forbid I should make so foul a shipwreck of my conscience, or leave so great a blot to my poor posterity, as to shed blood without law or warrant.

"Trusting that her majesty, of her accustomed clemency, and the rather by your good mediation, will take this my answer in good part, as proceeding from one who never will be inferior to any Christian subject living in honour, love, and obedience towards his sovereign, and thus I commit you to the mercy of the Almighty.

> "Your most assured poor friend,
> "A. POWLET (PAULET.)

"From Fotheringaye, the 2nd of February, 1586–7.

"P.S. – Your letters coming in the plural number, seem to be meant to sir Drue Drury as to myself, and yet because he is not named in them, neither the letter directed unto him, he forbeareth to make any particular answer, but subscribeth in heart to my opinion.

> "D. DRURY."

The next morning, Davison communicated these letters to his royal mistress, which having read, "her majesty," pursues Davison, "falling into terms of offence, complaining of 'the daintiness, and (as she called it) perjury of him and others, who, contrary to their oath of association, did cast the burden upon herself,' she rose up, and, after a turn or two, went into the gallery, whither I followed her; and there renewing her former speech, blaming 'the niceness of those precise fellows, (as she termed them,) who, in words, would do great things for her surety, but, indeed, perform nothing;' concluded by saying, 'that she could have it well enough done without them.' And here, entering into *particularities*, named unto me, as I remember, 'one Wingfield, who,' she assured me, 'would, with some others, undertake it,' which gave me occasion to shew unto her majesty how dishonourable, in my poor opinion, any such course would be, and how far she would be from shunning the blame and stain thereof, she so much sought to avoid; and so falling into the particular case of sir Amias Paulet and sir Drue Drury, discoursed unto her the great extremity she would have exposed those poor gentlemen to, for it, in a tender care of her surety, they should have done what she desired, she must either allow their act or disallow it. If she allowed it, she took the matter upon herself, with her infinite peril and dishonour; if she disallowed it, she should not only overthrow the gentlemen themselves, who had always truly and faithfully served and honoured her, but also their estates and posterities; besides the dishonour and injustice of such a course, which I humbly besought her majesty 'to consider of,' and so, after some little digression and speech about Mr. Secretary and others, touching some things passed heretofore, her majesty, calling to understand whether it were time to go to her closet, brake off our discourse."

"At my next access to her majesty, which, I take, was Tuesday, the day before my coming from court, I having certain things to be signed, her majesty entered of herself into some earnest discourse of the danger she daily lived in, and how it was more than time this matter were dispatched, swearing a great oath, 'that it was a shame for them all that it was not done;' and thereupon spake unto me, 'to have a letter written to Mr. Paulet for the despatch thereof, because the longer it was deferred, the more her danger increased;' whereunto, knowing what order had been taken by my lords in sending the commission to the earls, I answered, 'that I thought there was no necessity for such a letter, the warrant being so general and sufficient as it was.' Her majesty replied little else, 'but that she thought Mr. Paulet would look for it.'"

The entrance of one of her ladies, to hear her majesty's pleasure about dinner, broke off this conference, which took place on the very day of Mary's execution at Fotheringaye. It is a remarkable fact, withal, in the strangely linked history of these rival queens, that at the very time Elizabeth thundered out of her unfeminine execration against those who were (as she erroneously imagined) delaying the death of her hapless kinswoman, Mary was meekly imploring her Heavenly Father "to forgive all those who thirsted for her blood;" and lest this petition should be considered too general, she included the name of queen Elizabeth, in her dying prayer for her own son; not in the scornful spirit of the pharisee, but according to the divine precept of Him who has said, "Bless them that curse you, and pray for those that persecute you, and despitefully use you." What can be said, in illustration of the dispositions of these two queens, more striking than the simple record of this circumstance; which, remarkable as it is, appears to have escaped the attention of their biographers.

It may appear singular, that Davison did not endeavour to calm the ireful impatience of his sovereign, by apprising her that the deed was done; but Davison, being accustomed to her majesty's stormy temper, and characteristic dissimulation, suspected that she was as perfectly aware as himself of the bloody work, that had been performed in the hall of Fotheringaye castle that morning. He knew not how to believe, that the queen could be ignorant that the warrant had been sent down for that purpose, "considering," as he says, "who

the counsellors were by whom it was despatched."
One circumstance affords presumptive evidence
of Elizabeth's unconsciousness of this fact, which
is, that when the news of Mary's execution was
brought down to Greenwich early on the morning
of the 9th of February by Henry Talbot, not one
of her council would venture to declare it to her;
and it was actually concealed from her the whole of
that day, which she passed as if nothing remarkable
had happened.

In the morning, she went out on horseback
with her train, and after her return, she had a long
interview with Don Antonio, the claimant of the
crown of Portugal, whose title she supported for
the annoyance of her great political foe, Philip II. of
Spain. The whole day was, in fact, suffered to pass
away without one syllable of this important event
being communicated to her majesty by her ministers.
"In the evening," says Davison, "she learned the news
by other means." This was the general ringing of the
bells, and the blaze of bonfires that were universally
kindled in London and its vicinity, as the tidings
spread, and the majority of the people appeared
intoxicated with joy at what had taken place. Those
who inwardly mourned were compelled, by a
prudential regard for their own safety, to illuminate
their houses, and kindle bonfires like the rest.

The queen is said to have inquired the reason "why the bells rang out so merrily?" and was answered, "Because of the execution of the Scottish queen." Elizabeth received the news in silence. "Her majesty would not, at the first, seem to take any notice of it," says Davison, "but in the morning, falling into some heat and passion, she sent for Mr. Vice-chamberlain, (Hatton), to whom she disavowed the said execution, as a thing she never commanded nor intended, casting the burden generally on them all, but chiefly on my shoulders."

Camden tells us, "that as soon as the report of the death of the queen of Scots was brought to queen Elizabeth, she heard it with great indignation: her countenance altered; her speech faltered and failed her; and, through excessive sorrow, she stood in a manner astonished, insomuch that she gave herself over to passionate grief, putting herself into a mourning habit, and shedding abundance of tears. Her council she sharply rebuked, and commanded them out of her sight." Historians have, generally speaking, attributed Elizabeth's tears and lamentations, and the reproaches with which she overwhelmed her ministers on this occasion, to that profound hypocrisy which formed so prominent a feature in her character; but they may, with more truth, perhaps be attributed to the agonies of awakened conscience.

No sooner, indeed, was she assured that the crime which she had so long premeditated was actually perpetrated, than the horror of the act appears to have become apparent to herself, and she shrank from the idea of the personal odium she was likely to incur from the commission of so barbarous, so needless an outrage. If it had been a deed which could have been justified on the strong grounds of state necessity, "why," as sir Harris Nicolas has well observed, "should the queen have been so desirous of disavowing it?" Her conduct on this occasion resembles the mental cowardice of a guilty child, who, self-convicted and terrified at the prospect of disgrace and punishment, strives to shift the burden of his own fault on all who have been privy to the mischief, because they have not prevented him from the perpetration of the sin; yet Elizabeth's angry reproaches to her ministers were not undeserved on their parts, for deeply and subtilely had they played the tempters with their royal mistress, with regard to the unfortunate heiress of the crown. How systematically they alarmed her with the details of conspiracies against her life, and irritated her jealous temperament, by the repetition of every bitter sarcasm which had been elicited from her ill-treated rival, has been fully shewn.

Looking at the case in all its bearings, there is good reason to suppose that the anger which Elizabeth manifested, not only against her cautious dupe Davison, but Burleigh and his colleagues, was genuine. Davison clearly shews that they agreed to act upon their own responsibility, in despatching the warrant for Mary's execution, under the plausible pretext, that they thought it would be most agreeable to their royal mistress for them to take that course; they were also actuated by two very opposite fears – one was, that Elizabeth would disgrace both herself and them, by having Mary privily despatched in her prison; or, on the other hand, postpone the execution of the warrant from day to day, and possibly die herself in the interim – a contingency above all others to be prevented.

Elizabeth, therefore, it really ignorant of the resolution they had taken, was of course infuriated at their presuming to exercise the power of the crown, independently of her commands. The act would be of secondary importance in the eye of a sovereign of her jealous temperament; but the principle they had established, was alarming and offensive to the last degree. Ten men, calling themselves her servants, had constituted themselves a legislative body, *imperio in imperio*, to act by mutual consent, in one instance, independently of the authority of the sovereign; and had taken upon themselves to cause the head of an anointed queen to be stricken off by the common executioner. A dangerous precedent against royalty, which in process of time, encouraged a more numerous band of confederates to take away the life of their own sovereign, Charles I., in a manner equally illegal, and opposed to the spirit of the English constitution.

Personal hatred to Mary Stuart had not blinded Elizabeth to the possibility of the same principle being exercised against herself, on some future occasion; and, as far as she could, she testified her resentment against the whole junta, for the *lese majestæ* of which, they had been guilty, and, at the same time, endeavoured to escape the odium which the murder of her royal kinswoman was likely to bring on her, by flinging the whole burden of the crime on them.

Mr. Secretary Woolley writes the following brief particulars, to Leicester, of her majesty's deportment to such of her ministers who ventured to meet the first explosion of her wrath: "It pleased her majesty yesterday to call the lords and others of her council before her, into her withdrawing chamber, where she rebuked us all exceedingly, for our concealing from her our proceeding in the queen of Scots' case; but her indignation lighteth most on my lord-treasurer (Burleigh), and Mr. Davison, who called us together, and delivered the commission. For she protesteth, 'she gave express commandment to the contrary,' and therefore hath took order for the committing Mr. Secretary Davison to the Tower, if she continue this morning, in the mind she was yesternight, albeit, we all kneeled upon our knees to pray to the contrary. I think your lordship happy to be absent from these broils, and thought it my duty to let you understand them."

Woolley's letter is dated, "this present Sunday," by which we understand that the memorable interview between Elizabeth and her council did not take place, as generally asserted, immediately after she learned the tidings of Mary's execution on the Thursday evening, but on the Saturday. Burleigh she forbade her presence with every demonstration of serious displeasure. Walsingham came in for a share of her anger, on which he makes the following cynical comments to Leicester, which afford sufficient evidence of the irritation of both queen and cabinet at this crisis. "My very good lord, these sharp humours continue still, which doth greatly disquiet her majesty, and her poor servants that attend here. The lord-treasurer remaineth still in disgrace, and behind my back, her majesty giveth out very hard speeches of myself, which I the easier credit, for that I find in dealing with her, I am nothing gracious; and if her majesty could be otherwise served, I should not be used." Walsingham, goes on, after recounting matters of public business, to say, "The present discord between her majesty and her council, hindereth the necessary consultation that were to be desired for the preventing of the manifest perils that hang over this realm." He proceeds to state the queen's perversity in not allowing the necessary supplies for the Low Countries, and says, "her majesty doth wholly bend herself to devise some further means to disgrace her poor council that subscribed, and in respect thereof she neglected all other causes."

Elizabeth would probably have endeavoured to emancipate herself from Burleigh's political thraldom, if she had not found it impossible to weather out the storm that was gathering against her on the Spanish coast, without him. The veteran statesman was, besides, too firmly seated at the helm, to suffer himself to be driven from his office by a burst of female temper. He, the Talleyrand of the 16th century, understood the art of trimming his back to suit the gales from all points of the compass. While the tempest of Elizabeth's anger lasted, he lowered his sails, and affected the deepest penitence for having been so unfortunate as to displease her by his zeal for her service, and humiliated himself by writing the most abject letters that could be devised, and after a time succeeded in re-establishing his wonted ascendancy in the cabinet.

The luckless Davison was, meantime, selected as the scapegoat on whom the whole blame of the death of the Scottish queen was to be laid. He was stripped of his offices, sent to the Tower, and subjected to a Star-Chamber process, for the double contempt of revealing the secret communications which had passed between her majesty and him, to others of her ministers; this was doubtless the head and front of his offending, and the real cause for which he was punished; the other misdemeanour was giving up to them the warrant which had been committed to his special trust. His principal defence consisted in repeated appeals to the conscience of the queen, "with whom," he said, "it did not become him to contend." He was sentenced to pay a fine of ten thousand pounds, and to suffer imprisonment during her majesty's pleasure.

This dark chapter of the annals of the maiden monarch closed with the farce of her assuming the office of chief mourner, at the funeral of her royal victim, when the mangled remains of Mary Stuart, after being permitted to lie unburied, and neglected for six months, were, at last, interred, with regal pomp, in Peterborough Cathedral, attended by a train of nobles, and ladies of the highest rank, in the English court. The countess of Bedford acted as queen Elizabeth's proxy on that occasion, and made the offering in her name. "What a glorious princess!" exclaimed the sarcastic pontiff, Sixtus V., when the news reached the Vatican, – "it is a pity," he added, "that Elizabeth and I cannot marry, our children would have mastered the whole world."